DATE DUE		

—Diseases and People—

SICKLE CELL ANEMIA

Alvin and Virginia Silverstein
and Laura Silverstein Nunn

Enslow Publishers, Inc.

40 Industrial Road	PO Box 38
Box 398	Aldershot
Berkeley Heights, NJ 07922	Hants GU12 6BP
USA	UK

http://www.enslow.com

Library of Congress Cataloging-in-Publication Data

Silverstein, Alvin.
    Sickle cell anemia / Alvin and Virginia Silverstein and Laura Silverstein Nunn.
       p. cm.— (Diseases and People)
    Includes bibliographical references and index.
    Summary: Explores the history of sickle cell anemia, discussing its symptoms,
diagnosis, and treatment.
    ISBN 0-89490-711-5
    1. Sickle cell anemia—Juvenile literature. [1. Sickle cell anemia. 2. Diseases.]
I. Silverstein, Virginia B. II. Nunn, Laura Silverstein. III. Title. IV. Series.
RC641.7.S5S57   1997
616.1'527—dc20
                                                    96-22643
                                                       CIP
                                                       AC

Printed in the United States of America

10 9 8 7 6 5 4

Illustration Credits:
Courtesy of Sophie Xyloportas and the AHEPA Cooley's Anemia Foundation,
p. 37; Dith Pran/*New York Times* Pictures, p. 35; March of Dimes Birth Defects
Foundation, pp. 45, 69; National Institutes of Health, pp. 75, 86; National
Medical Library, p. 13; New Jersey Newsphotos, pp. 43, 55; Northern California
Comprehensive Sickle Cell Center, pp. 21, 24, 27; Photo by Louis A. Sapienza,
courtesy of Muhlenberg Regional Medical Center, Plainfield, N.J., p. 66; Scott
Anger/*New York Times* Pictures, p. 49; United States Public Health Service, p. 50;
UPI/Bettmann, pp. 6, 16.

Cover Illustration:
Photo by Louis A. Sapienza, courtesy of Muhlenberg Regional Medical Center,
Plainfield, N.J.

Contents

Acknowledgments

The authors are grateful to Dr. Oswaldo Castro, director of the Center for Sickle Cell Disease, Howard University, Washington, D.C., and Renee Y. Cecil, R.N., B.S.N., nurse coordinator at the Comprehensive Sickle Cell Center, The Children's Hospital of Philadelphia, for their careful reading of the manuscript and their many helpful comments and suggestions. Thanks also to Karen Duggins for her insights into sickle cell disease from the patient's viewpoint.

SICKLE CELL DISEASE

What is it? A hereditary disorder affecting hemoglobin, the oxygen-carrying substance in red blood cells. The altered hemoglobin tends to form polymers that make the red cells stiff and fragile. These sickled cells may block small blood vessels, starving the tissues they feed.

Who gets it? Although commonly known as a "black disease" and most frequently seen in Africans and African Americans, it is also found in people from the Mediterranean region, the Caribbean, the Middle East, and India.

How do you get it? By inheriting two genes for the abnormal hemoglobin, one from each parent. It is not contagious and is not transmitted by germs.

What are the symptoms? Tiredness, jaundice, painfully swollen hands and feet, enlarged spleen, pains in the joints, more severe colds and other infections, slowed growth, and periodic episodes of intense pain.

How is it treated? Daily oral penicillin and immunization against pneumonia now help protect children with sickle cell anemia from dangerous infections. Painkillers and rehydration help ease episodes. Drugs such as hydroxyurea and butyrate can promote the production of fetal hemoglobin and prevent sickling.

How can it be prevented? Newborn screening programs are aimed at early identification to prevent serious symptoms and infection; screening and counseling of young adults and prenatal diagnosis can aid in family planning to avoid the birth of affected children.

Jesse Jackson at the First National Black Political Convention in Gary, Indiana, on March 3, 1972. Like many other African Americans, Jackson carries the sickle cell trait.

A Crisis in the Blood

Reverend Jesse Jackson, a civil rights activist, has always been a man with strong ambition. After Martin Luther King, Jr.'s, assassination in April 1968, Jackson followed in King's footsteps, continuing the fight for the rights of African Americans. All that year, he led marches and made speeches. Nothing stood in his way. He seemed unstoppable—until December.

In December 1968, Jesse Jackson led a crusade against construction companies, trying to force them to hire African-American workers. Jackson and his group were then arrested for picketing outside one of the construction sites. As Jackson was about to be released from jail, he collapsed and was rushed to the hospital. He was suffering from mononucleosis, but in routine blood tests, doctors discovered that Jackson was carrying the sickle cell trait. He decided to go public with this medical matter to help call attention to the problem and promote greater awareness and understanding of sickle cell disease.[1]

Sickle cell anemia, also known as sickle cell disease, has been around for centuries. Years ago, little was known about this mysterious illness, except that it was taking the lives of so many people throughout the world. It had no name, no known cause, and no treatment. It was not until the beginning of the twentieth century that research on this unusual illness was finally started and some long-standing questions were answered.

During the 1970s, the federal government finally acknowledged sickle cell disease as a serious illness that needs attention. Before much was known about sickle cell anemia, people considered it a "black disease" because it affected mostly Africans and African Americans, although it could occur in other races. Nationwide sickle cell screening programs were started, but lawmakers concentrated only on African Americans. Many African Americans felt that their race was being targeted and that instead of helping them the screening programs were making sickle cell disease an additional excuse for discrimination against their race.

Sickle cell anemia is an inherited blood disorder that occurs in people who have inherited an abnormal gene from both parents. This gene controls the production of hemoglobin, the chemical that gives blood its red color. The abnormal form of the hemoglobin gene causes the red blood cells to change from their normal, round shape to a long, curved shape that looks like the blade of a sickle—hence its name. Normal red blood cells are flexible and squeeze through the smallest blood vessels with ease, but sickle cells become sticky and stiff and cannot fit through the narrowest capillaries. They tend to clump together and clog up the blood vessels, reducing the flow of oxygen and food materials to the body's cells.

People with sickle cell anemia often experience painful crises, or episodes of intense pain. The sickling of the red blood cells causes these pain episodes. Sometimes the pain becomes so unbearable that sickle cell sufferers need to be hospitalized.

For a long time, the only treatments for sickle cell anemia were emergency measures to help get people through the episodes. Painkillers, blood transfusions, or fluids dripped through a hollow needle directly into a vein could provide some relief. Recently, however, effective methods have been developed to help prevent sickle cell episodes and permit people with the disease to lead a more normal life. One approach has focused on drugs that step up the body's production of fetal hemoglobin, the main form that is present in the blood from before birth until about six months after birth.

With better diagnosis and more effective treatments, the life expectancy of people with sickle cell anemia has increased dramatically over the past two decades. In the 1970s, only about half of those who were diagnosed could expect to survive to adulthood. A 1994 study by Dr. Orah Platt of Children's Hospital in Boston, following up 3,764 people, found that more than half were living at least into their forties—and the oldest people in the study were well into their sixties.[2]

At present, there is no known cure for sickle cell disease. However, there is hope for the future. Researchers are working on forms of gene therapy that will enable people with the disease to produce normal red blood cells.

Sickle Cell Disease in History

In 1904, Dr. James B. Herrick, a Chicago physician, treated a twenty-year-old college student from the West Indian island of Grenada. This young man came to Dr. Herrick with complaints of shortness of breath, heart palpitations, abdominal pain, and aches and pains in his muscles. He also felt tired all the time, had headaches, experienced attacks of dizziness, and had ulcers on his legs. After noting all of these symptoms, Dr. Herrick took a sample of the man's blood and viewed it under a microscope. He expected to see tiny, round red blood cells, but instead, this man's red blood cells were long and curved. The cells looked like the blade of a sickle. The man's original diagnosis was anemia, a severe reduction in red blood cells, but this unusual microscopic finding was not like any kind of anemia Dr. Herrick had ever seen before. The doctor spent the next six years studying this strange disease and treated his patient as best he could. In 1910, Dr. Herrick wrote up his observations and became the first person to publish a medical report on the new condition that was later named sickle cell anemia.[1]

Over the following years, other doctors observed patients who had similar symptoms. As the reports accumulated, a definite pattern began to emerge. Most of the sickle cell patients were black, and the disease appeared to be hereditary, often occurring in both parents and children or in several children in the same family. Eventually, hundreds of cases of the sickle cell disease turned up, and doctors realized that this unusual illness affected millions![2]

Sickle Cell Disease Takes on Two Forms

In 1926, Dr. Thomas P. Cooley and Dr. P. Lee did more extensive studies on sickle cell disease. They described the most serious form of sickle cell disease as sickle cell anemia. People in this category have severely sickled cells and often experience unbearable pain, which sometimes leads to hospitalization. People who have sickle cell trait carry the sickle cell gene but do not have the actual disease. These people rarely experience symptoms because they have too few sickled cells to have an effect on the body. People with sickle cell trait can live long, productive lives without any ill effects of the disease.[3]

In 1910, James B. Herrick was the first person to publish a medical report on sickle cell anemia.

AN OLD SCOURGE

Sickle cell disease may not have been named until the early 1900s, but it has long been a fact of life for people in Africa and the Mediterranean region. Parents watched helplessly while some of their children, who had seemed perfectly healthy, died suddenly for no apparent reason, and others developed swollen joints that had them screaming with pain. "Even our illiterate great grandparents knew the sickle cell crisis," remarked one doctor in Ghana.[4] Many tribal names for the disease, such as chwechweechwe, nuiduidui, and ahututuo, are imitations of the cries and moans of the sufferers or phrases like "body chewing" or "body biting," which describe their terrible torment.[5] In one West African tribe, children who died soon after birth were called ogbanjes, meaning "children who come and go." The tribespeople believed that an evil spirit was trying to be born into a family with ogbanje children, but the babies bravely died to save the family from the demon.[6]

A Chance Meeting Leads to Discovery

In 1945, two Nobel-prizewinners, Dr. William B. Castle, an expert on anemias, and Dr. Linus Pauling, a noted physical chemist, took a train ride together and happened to talk about sickle cell anemia. Castle told Pauling about how the cells in sickle cell patients sickled when oxygen levels were low. Pauling thought that hemoglobin, a chemical in red blood cells that carries oxygen, might be the key.

Intrigued by this conversation, Dr. Pauling did further research on sickle cell disease. He found that an abnormal form of hemoglobin was indeed responsible for the sickling in sickle cell patients. It is when the cells change their shape that they become sticky and clamp onto one another. Some of these abnormal blood cells are destroyed in the spleen, causing anemia. Others clog up the blood vessels, causing tissue damage and pain.[7]

Soon Dr. Pauling was able to determine which people had the sickle cell trait and which had sickle cell disease. He used a technique for separating chemicals, called electrophoresis. A small sample of a mixture is placed on a gel-coated microscope slide, which is then placed in an electric field. Different chemicals in the mixture move along the gel at different rates, depending on their electrical charges. Eventually they are separated into distinct spots or bands on the gel. The normal and abnormal forms of hemoglobin have slightly different electrical charges and therefore can be separated by electrophoresis. So by taking a few drops of blood and placing the sample in an electric field, Dr. Pauling was able to test for sickle hemoglobin.

Linus Pauling was a pioneer in sickle cell disease research.

(The blood of people with sickle cell trait contains a mixture of normal and abnormal hemoglobin.)[8]

One Tiny Change Is to Blame

In 1956, another scientist, Dr. Vernon Ingram, used Dr. Pauling's tests to find a key difference between normal and abnormal hemoglobin. Like other proteins, hemoglobin is made up of chains of smaller chemical building blocks, amino acids; these chains are folded and looped into a complicated structure. Dr. Ingram used enzymes and other chemicals to break some of the bonds in the hemoglobin molecule, converting it to a mixture of shorter amino acid chains. By separating these fragments and sorting them out, it is possible to work out a map of the protein's structure. After comparing a normal hemoglobin molecule to an abnormal one, Dr. Ingram discovered that the two proteins had different amino acids in one spot on the chain. That single tiny change in the hemoglobin molecule seemed to be the cause of the sickling.[9] It seems amazing that such a small difference could cause so many harmful effects in the body, but gradually researchers worked out exactly how it does the damage. Sickle cell anemia was the first hereditary disease for which the molecular cause was determined.

3

What Is Sickle Cell Disease?

Twin boys Alex and Aaron were nearly three years old when tests showed that they had sickle cell anemia. Neither of them had ever shown any symptoms of the disease, but just two months later Alex had his first sickle cell episode. It started with an ordinary cold; then, suddenly, Alex was crying with pain so severe that he was rushed to the hospital. There the tiny patient had a stroke that caused massive damage to his brain. His mother remembers that there were so many monitors and tubes attached to him that "there was just one little spot on his leg that I could kiss." Five days later, Alex died. Then, exactly a month after Alex was taken to the hospital, Aaron had a sickle cell episode, too. His mother was terrified, but Aaron recovered quickly and was soon home again. Over the next four years, he was hospitalized seven more times, but his mother considers him lucky—many other children with sickle cell anemia are hospitalized twice as often in just one year.[1]

Twenty-year-old Sutanna spent the greater part of her childhood in and out of hospitals. She has sickle cell anemia. She often felt the painful, aching feeling was more than she could bear. At times, her arms and legs swelled so badly she could not even walk and had to spend weeks at a time in the hospital. But now Sutanna is hospitalized only two or three times a year. She views this as "not all that bad," considering what her life was like while she was growing up.[2]

Nineteen-year-old Donna was no stranger to hospitals. In one of her sickle cell episodes, Donna found herself lying on a hospital stretcher with an oxygen mask strapped to her face. She was hooked up to an IV, just waiting for the painkiller to take effect. As Donna was being examined, she noticed that she was having episode pain in her hip. This was unusual—the pain was usually in her arm or her back. After a number of tests, it was found that the pain in her hip was not just another sickle cell episode. It was more serious than that. Donna had a bacterial infection in her bone, called osteomyelitis, which required six weeks of intravenous antibiotics. With the proper medical treatment, Donna could overcome this—until the next medical crisis.[3]

Who Has Sickle Cell Disease?

Today more than sixty thousand Americans have sickle cell anemia, and an estimated 2.5 million are carrying the sickle cell trait. These figures include African Americans, Greek Americans, Italian Americans, and Puerto Ricans. Although sickle cell disease is widespread, it affects mostly blacks. An estimated 1 in 375 African Americans have sickle cell disease, and 1 in 12 have the sickle cell trait.[4]

Sickle cell anemia has long been widespread in Africa, especially in West Africa. (In some areas, 40 percent of the population carry the sickle cell trait.)[5] Scientists believe that genetic changes (mutations) leading to sickle cell disease arose in several different parts of Africa as much as fifty thousand years ago; separate mutations with a similar result also occurred in India or Arabia. The mutant genes were carried along as people migrated from one place to another. The slave trade helped to spread sickle cell genes to northern Africa and Europe and later to the lands of the Western hemisphere. Today sickle cell disease is found in Africa, the United States, Latin America, the Caribbean, India, Saudi Arabia, and some of the Mediterranean countries of Europe such as Italy and Greece.

What Causes Sickle Cell Anemia?

Sickle cell anemia is a genetic blood disorder. This means that it is not contagious. There are no "sickle cell germs." You cannot "catch" the disease from someone who has it, the way you can catch a cold. You cannot get it from touching or kissing, from someone sneezing on you, or even by coming in contact with the blood of someone who has the disease. The

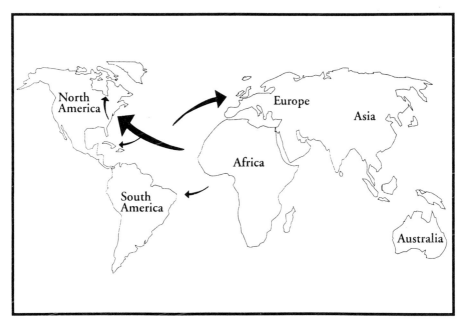

Today, sickle cell disease is found in Africa, the United States, Latin America, the Caribbean, India, Saudi Arabia, and some countries of the Mediterranean, such as Italy and Greece.

HOW DO WE INHERIT OUR TRAITS?

The blueprints for the human body are chemically coded in units called genes. Our genes determine traits such as hair color, eye color, and bone structure. The genes are lined up like beads on a necklace on structures called chromosomes. A complete set of chromosomes (forty-six in humans) is found in each body cell. Chromosomes come in pairs, and there are usually at least two genes for each trait, one inherited from each parent. Some genes are dominant: Their effects are seen even if only one of the particular gene is present. Some genes are recessive: Their effects appear only if two recessive genes are inherited, one from each parent. Sickle cell anemia, for example, is caused by a recessive gene for an abnormal form of hemoglobin.

only way you can get any form of sickle cell disease is by inheriting sickle cell genes from your parents.

It takes a double dose of sickle cell genes—one inherited from each parent—to produce sickle cell anemia. A child who has inherited only one sickle cell gene has what is called sickle cell trait. People who have the sickle cell gene are called carriers.

Carriers of the sickle cell trait experience no symptoms of the disease. Both carriers and people with the disease have sickle hemoglobin, but carriers may have about 30 percent, whereas a person with sickle cell anemia may have 80 percent or more sickle hemoglobin. Carriers can live long, productive lives without any disturbance from the disease. However, studies have shown that rare conditions such as extreme stress, lack of oxygen, a high altitude, or dehydration after physical exercise may be triggers that make the red blood cells sickle. Carriers should also be aware that their sickle cell trait can be passed on to their children.

Here are the probabilities that a child of a particular couple will develop sickle cell anemia or carry the sickle cell trait:

- If both parents are sickle cell carriers, there is a 25 percent chance that their child will have sickle cell anemia, a 50 percent chance that the child will be a carrier, and a 25 percent chance that the child will have only normal hemoglobin.

- If one parent is a carrier and the other is not, each of their children has a 50 percent chance of inheriting a sickle cell gene, that is, of being a carrier of the sickle cell trait, and a

When both parents have a hemoglobin trait:

When only one of the parents has a hemoglobin trait:

Sickle Cell Disease
(SS)

Sickle Cell Trait
(AS)

Sickle Cell Trait
(AS)

Sickle Cell Trait
(AS)

Sickle Cell Trait
(AS)

No Trait
(AA)

Sickle Cell Trait
(AS)

Sickle Cell Trait
(AS)

Sickle Cell Trait
(AS)

No Trait
(AA)

No Trait
(AA)

No Trait
(AA)

It takes a double dose of sickle cell genes, one inherited from each parent, to produce sickle cell anemia.

50 percent chance of having only normal hemoglobin. None will have sickle cell anemia.

When a person inherits a defective sickle cell gene from both parents, many of the red blood cells change their form from a normal, rounded shape to a long, curved shape. These deformed cells (sickled cells) have a short life span and quickly die off, faster than new cells can be created. The number of red blood cells in the body is then reduced, causing the person to become weak and anemic.

What Our Blood Does

Blood is actually a complex mixture of chemicals and cells suspended in a watery fluid. It carries materials from one part of the body to another. One of its crucial jobs is to transport oxygen from the lungs, where this gas is absorbed from the inhaled air, to all the body cells. Oxygen is needed for the energy-producing reactions that power all the body's activities. Each time you move a muscle, digest a meal, or even think, oxygen-using reactions supply the power for your actions.

Oxygen is carried in the blood mainly by the red blood cells. (Small amounts are also dissolved in the watery part of the blood.) There are 25 trillion red blood cells circulating through an adult's body. A single drop of blood contains more than 250 million red blood cells. Their normal working life span is about four months; old, worn-out red cells are broken down in the liver and spleen, and their chemicals are recycled. Each second, from 2 to 10 million red blood cells in a person's body are destroyed, and an equal number of new red cells are produced in his or her bone marrow to replace them.

Normal red blood cells are shaped like doughnuts with the centers only partly scooped out. Typically, they are all the same size and perfectly round. The red cells are small—about 0.0002 inch (7.5 micrometers) in diameter. Yet they are larger than the smallest capillaries, which are only 0.00013 inch (5 micrometers) wide—less than one-twentieth the width of a hair. But these red blood cells are soft and flexible, so they can bend and twist as they pass single file through the capillaries of the body.

Each red blood cell contains a red pigment called hemoglobin. The "heme" in hemoglobin is an iron-containing chemical, and "globin" refers to a type of protein that is combined with heme. We need a source of iron in our diet to provide for new hemoglobin production. Hemoglobin can combine chemically with oxygen but also releases it fairly readily; it can also form a similar compound with carbon dioxide, the cells' main waste product. When the red blood cells pass through the capillaries in the lungs, they pick up oxygen from the inhaled air and release the carbon dioxide they have gathered from the body cells. Then, passing through the circulatory system, they carry oxygen to all the vital organs.

Sickle cell anemia occurs when an abnormal form of hemoglobin, Hb S, is produced. The Hb S molecules can bind oxygen just as well as the normal hemoglobin, but when the oxygen concentration is low, Hb S molecules join together, forming stiff fibers. The fibers distort the shape of the red

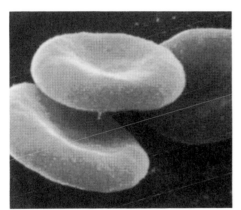 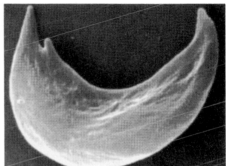

Normal blood cells are doughnut-shaped, but when an abnormal form of hemoglobin (Hb S) is produced, the cells appear sickle-shaped.

blood cells, making them long and curved, like a crescent moon. These sickle cells cannot bend and twist the way normal red cells can, and they are unable to squeeze through the tiny capillaries. Repeated sickling also makes the cells weak, and they survive considerably less than the normal 120-day life span. When they die, a shortage of red blood cells develops, resulting in anemia.

Anemia

Anemia is a condition that develops when the number of red blood cells falls below the normal level. It may also refer to a low amount of hemoglobin, making it impossible to carry enough oxygen to the body's tissues. People who are anemic often feel tired and weak.

Anemia can occur for a number of reasons. It may happen when the body does not produce enough red blood cells. It may occur when someone loses a lot of blood. Anemia may also develop because of a deficiency of iron, vitamin B_{12}, or folic acid in the diet. Certain drugs can bring on anemia. Anemia is also sometimes the sign of an illness, like arthritis, or a major disease, like cancer.

There are various types of anemias. One kind, called pernicious anemia, occurs when the body is unable to absorb vitamin B_{12} from food properly. (This vitamin is essential for building red blood cells.) In this case, B_{12} injections may be necessary to correct the problem.

Aplastic anemia develops when the bone marrow becomes unable to produce red blood cells. There is often no known

FORMS OF HEMOGLOBIN

The form of hemoglobin normally found in adults (Hb A) consists of four long chains of amino acid units. Two of these globin chains, the alpha chains, each have 141 amino acid units. The other two, the beta chains, each have 146 amino acid units. Sickle cell anemia occurs when there is a chemical change in the hemoglobin gene, resulting in a slightly different protein, Hb S. One specific amino acid on each beta chain is changed into another, while both of the alpha chains stay the same. This "simple" substitution of just one amino acid out of 146 produces a major change in the electrical charge of that part of the molecule and alters its behavior.

Actually, more than three hundred different kinds of abnormal hemoglobin have been observed, and a few of them can cause sickling. Hb S is the most common sickle cell hemoglobin in Africa, but another abnormal form, Hb C, is also found there. This form has a different amino acid substitution in the same spot on the beta chain and can cause a milder form of anemia. In Southeast Asia, Hb E is the most common abnormal hemoglobin and causes an even milder anemia.

cause for this condition. It is usually treated by regular blood transfusions until the bone marrow starts to function normally again. However, in many cases, the bone marrow never recovers, and the person dies.

Hemolytic anemia occurs when the red blood cells are destroyed in the liver and spleen faster than they are produced. This condition may be inherited or it may be acquired—for example, when the red blood cells are damaged due to severe burns or freezing, or sometimes following infections. Hereditary causes of hemolytic anemia include sickle cell anemia.

A Unique Disease

Sickle cell anemia is like no other disease. It is hard to make generalizations about this illness because the symptoms vary from person to person. Although one common complaint of people with sickle cell anemia is the unbearable pain, even the pain is unique. The pain may be very severe for one person and mild for another. (The cause of this difference is not known. It may be a greater tendency for the red cells to sickle.) The pain may strike different parts of the body for different people. In fact, symptoms may even vary within the same person.

Sickle cell sufferers have said that the pain of their episodes is worse than the pain of cancer, childbirth, or arthritis. The symptoms are not only difficult to manage, but they are also lifelong and may be crippling.

TALE OF THE SPLEEN

"She went to bed one night and her tummy was hurting her. And the next morning . . . her stomach was really big, like when you see people in Africa who haven't been eating. It was really big and real hard. So I rushed her to the hospital . . . And she was in a lot of pain, a lot of pain! She would run high-grade fevers of 103, she wouldn't eat or drink, she had a hardness in the stomach and pains in her legs . . . they found out she had an enlarged spleen. . . . that's what makes her stomach real, real hard—I mean her stomach gets as hard as this table. And if you touch it, or she moves, she just screams."—a mother talking about her two-year-old daughter.[6]

The spleen plays a very important role in protecting children from infections. It is packed with disease-fighting cells that can produce antibodies and other natural defenses against germs. Sickled cells may become trapped in the spleen, blocking tiny blood vessels and resulting in damage to the tissues they nourish. Fibrous scar tissue gradually replaces the spleen's working tissues, making it less able to fight infection. The blockage of spleen blood vessels may also cause the spleen to enlarge, filling the whole abdominal cavity, as blood is trapped inside it.

People with sickle cell anemia may develop jaundice, in which the skin and the whites of the eyes have a yellowish tint. (This condition is not harmful itself, but it is a sign of abnormality in the blood. When accompanied by nausea, vomiting, and abdominal pain, jaundice may indicate gall bladder problems.)

Some sufferers develop leg ulcers, which are sores that do not heal. These sores are usually seen in adults; they are brought on by poor circulation and typically occur on the ankles. Poor circulation is also the cause of the painful joints that afflict older people with sickle cell disease. The blood supply to the hip joints, in particular, may become so poor that the bone dies and must be replaced by an artificial hip joint. Impaired circulation to the eyes can be severe and may even cause blindness.

A very common symptom in young children is the hand-foot syndrome: As tiny blood vessels are blocked by sickled cells, the hands and feet swell and become hot, red, and painful. Children may also grow more slowly than normal so that they are typically small for their age, with an underdeveloped body. They also may have more severe colds and sore throats. A hard, enlarged spleen is another common symptom in children.

The most characteristic symptom of sickle cell anemia is the sickle cell episode. People usually experience severe pain in the chest, abdomen, arms, and legs. The pain can last for hours or even weeks and may occur several times a year.

Sickle Cell Episodes

When the sickled cells get stuck in the blood vessels, they form logjams that plug up the capillaries and prevent the oxygen-carrying blood from flowing to all the vital organs. Tissues "downstream" from the blockage are starved of oxygen and nutrients; meanwhile, other red blood cells cannot make it through, and without oxygen, they also start to sickle. The resulting sickle cell episodes are periods of pain attacks. They can be mild or severe.

Sickle cell episodes are very unpredictable. The pain can develop in any organ or joint in the body. The symptoms vary greatly from person to person and even within the same person. One person may have only one episode a year, while another may have one every few weeks. Or a person may go for months or years without an episode and then suddenly have one after another. Dr. Kenny Cooper, a Wilmington, Delaware, internist, notes that a sickle cell episode generally happens when the body is under stress.[7] It might be brought on by a chest cold or some other infection in the body, for example. Some patients report that an episode occurred after they went swimming, or when the weather suddenly turned bad.

Sickle cell episodes can produce disastrous effects. The lack of oxygen can damage vital organs such as the lungs, kidneys, and spleen. Narrowing and blockage of blood vessels in the brain due to sickle cell episodes can cause a stroke that may result in paralysis or other disabilities. Patients are also very vulnerable to infections.

Older people with sickle cell anemia may develop chronic pain. Dr. Dorothy C. Moore, a doctor in her forties who has the disease, comments:

> I had my most severe painful episodes when I was younger, but it has evolved into a chronic type of pain that I have just about all the time. It's similar to acute arthritis, but instead of just my joints hurting, the whole bone itself hurts. . . . When I feel it coming on, I try to engross myself in my work and ward it off. I don't always succeed.[8]

Chronic pain can make life a misery, but it is not just a quality-of-life problem. A study of more than thirty-five hundred sickle cell patients conducted in 1991 by the Sickle Cell Disease branch of the National Heart, Lung and Blood Institute found that people with three or more pain episodes a year tended to die earlier than those who had episodes less often.[9]

Thalassemia, the Mediterranean Disease

Thalassemia, like sickle cell anemia, is a group of hereditary disorders affecting the hemoglobin in the red blood cells. It occurs when the body does not produce enough of one of the hemoglobin chains. Anemia develops because there is not enough working hemoglobin to keep the body's organs well supplied with oxygen. Meanwhile, the part of the molecule that is produced normally builds up inside the red blood cells, damaging their membranes and shortening their life span. Thalassemia usually affects people from areas surrounding the Mediterranean Sea. In fact, its name comes from *thalassa*, the

Dorothy C. Moore, a doctor who herself has sickle cell disease, suffers from chronic pain.

ancient Greek word for "sea." This disease also occurs in the Middle East and in parts of Africa and Asia.

Symptoms of thalassemia usually include tiredness, irritability, pale skin, poor appetite, and distorted growth. A child may develop an enlarged heart, liver, and spleen.

Thalassemia is the result of defects in the alpha or beta chains of the hemoglobin molecule. In alpha-thalassemia, the production of the alpha chains is reduced or absent; when there is little or no production of beta chains, the disease is called beta-thalassemia. Beta-thalassemia is the most common type in the Mediterranean area, and alpha-thalassemia in Southeast Asia.

The most severe form of thalassemia is called thalassemia major, also known as Cooley's anemia, named after Dr. Thomas Cooley. It occurs when the genetic defect is inherited from both parents. Thalassemia major sufferers may die in infancy if not properly treated. A milder form, called thalassemia intermedia, occurs when a severe form of the defect is inherited from one parent or the mild form is inherited from both. It is usually not fatal. The mildest form is called thalassemia minor. It occurs when the defect is inherited from only one parent. People with this form are called carriers of the disease because they do not experience any symptoms but may pass it on to their children. Thalassemia genes may also be combined with sickle cell genes, causing disorders of varying severity.

Mia Xyloportas, the AHEPA Cooley's Anemia poster child, was born with beta-thalassemia. From the age of six months she received blood transfusions about once a month; when she was four (shown above), chelation therapy was added. A happy, active child, Mia never minded the treatments. When she was five, a bone marrow transplant cured her, and she no longer needs treatments.

The Malaria Connection

Why would genes as harmful as sickle cell or thalassemia be so widespread in many populations? It might seem that a mutation that killed or crippled many of its carriers would tend not to be passed on to very many children and would gradually disappear. For a long time, scientists have speculated on possible explanations. Perhaps there is some compensating benefit, they theorized. An English neurologist, Lord Brain, for example, once suggested that although a double dose of the sickle cell gene could be fatal, a single gene might increase a person's resistance to a disease. As more research was done, it was discovered that he was right. The disease is malaria.

A British geneticist, J. B. S. Haldane, noticed that malaria was very common in the Mediterranean area, where so many people carried the thalassemia gene. From this, he speculated that people who have this gene may have a resistance to malaria. Scientists began to research this theory and discovered that not only was Haldane right, it also applied to the sickle cell gene, too.

Malaria is caused by a microscopic parasite that lives inside red blood cells. The parasite is carried by one type of mosquito found in the tropics, especially in Africa. When the insect bites people, it injects malaria microbes into them. The mosquito goes from person to person, spreading this potentially fatal disease.

Only people with sickle cell trait, not the illness itself, are protected against malaria. People with sickle cell anemia would either die from the blood disorder or die after coming

38

into contact with malaria because of their weakened immune systems. However, when someone with sickle cell trait is bitten by a mosquito carrying the malaria parasite, the person's body is somehow shielded from this deadly disease. Scientists have found that the red blood cells of people with sickle cell trait break down quickly when the malaria parasite attacks them. Since the parasite must grow inside red blood cells, the disease does not have a chance to get firmly established in the bodies of these sickle cell carriers.

However, not everyone with the sickle cell trait is protected against malaria. Apparently, resistance to the disease occurs only in children between the ages of two and four. Adults with

 TRACING THEIR ROOTS

Because their ancestors were brought to the New World as slaves, many African Americans have no written records of their origins. They may not know where their African ancestors lived. But because researchers have established which kinds of hemoglobin genes are found in various parts of Africa, blood samples can provide valuable clues. For example, genetic studies of African Americans in Baltimore have suggested that about 18 percent of their ancestors came from Bantu Africa, 15 percent from the West African coast, and 62 percent from central West Africa.[10]

the trait can fall victim to malaria the same as people without the trait. Still, the increased survival of children carrying the sickle cell gene in areas where malaria is a major health problem is enough to give the gene an advantage.

When malaria spreads through a village of sickle cell carriers, those without the sickle cell trait usually die and the ones with the trait live on. They are then able to grow up and pass on the sickle cell gene to their children. Over hundreds and thousands of years, as the survivors had children with the sickle cell trait, millions became protected from malaria.

Thus, the areas with heavy malaria were the same as the heavy sickle cell areas. Where there was more malaria, there was more sickle cell. Where there was less malaria, the sickle cell gene was relatively rare. Worldwide, sickle cell genetics is an interesting example of evolution in action. Studies have found that African Americans, who have lived in malaria-free areas for as long as ten generations, have lower sickle cell gene frequencies than Africans—and the frequencies have dropped more than those of other, less harmful African genes. Similarly, the sickle cell gene is less common among blacks in Curaçao, a malaria-free island in the Caribbean, than in Surinam, a neighboring island where malaria is rampant—even though the ancestors of both populations came from the same region of Africa.[11]

Diagnosis

4

N ellie Thomas remembers comforting her baby, George, through his continuous screams of pain. They had started just a few weeks after he was born about half a century ago. None of the doctors she consulted at the local hospitals in Newark, New Jersey, could give her any explanations for her son's misery. Nellie recalls that many times George's tiny body became so stiff that she could not even bend his arms and legs; during one attack, his foot was bent almost backwards. What kind of illness could have such a frightening effect on such a young child?

The doctors did not know what was wrong with George, but they felt sure he would not survive. "They told me he wouldn't live to be four years old, then they said he wouldn't live to be five," Nellie says. Finally, a German doctor, visiting Newark for a medical conference, made an accurate diagnosis of George's illness. It was sickle cell anemia.

In the years that followed, George continued to have painful sickle cell episodes and was hospitalized many times, but he managed to live a relatively normal life. He did not start school until he was past seven, because school officials thought he would not be able to keep up, but he eventually graduated from high school with honors. The disease took its toll, though, and George died at the age of forty.

Things are quite different today for George's grand-niece, Rabiyyah, who also has sickle cell anemia. Much more is known about the disease now; there are accurate tests that can give a prompt diagnosis and effective treatments that ease suffering and prevent dangerous complications. Rabiyyah can look forward to a much longer life with far less suffering.[1]

Early Diagnosis Is Important

Since there are so many different complications resulting from sickle cell anemia, doctors may be fooled into thinking that abdominal pain, for instance, may be a sign of a bleeding ulcer or appendicitis. This misdiagnosis could lead to unnecessary surgery.

An early diagnosis is very important. However, symptoms of the disease may not appear until the child is at least four to six months of age. Fortunately, there are ways to test for sickle cell anemia even before any symptoms begin to show up.

Rabiyyah Quiddus (shown with her mother, Adilah) has sickle cell anemia, but treatment for her is much better today than it was for her great uncle, George Thomas.

There are also tests for sickle cell trait to aid people in making important family decisions.

Over the years, various tests have been used to diagnose sickle cell disease, but some tests are favored by physicians and are more widely used.

The Sodium Metabisulfite Test

One test that is fairly simple and rather inexpensive to perform is the sodium metabisulfite test. A drop of blood is put on a glass slide with a drop of the chemical sodium metabisulfite. The slide is covered with a coverslip and sealed with vaseline to keep out oxygen. After a short time, technicians check for sickling. Unfortunately, this test cannot distinguish between sickle cell anemia and sickle cell trait. Also, it may also produce false negatives and false positives, and it is not reliable in testing newborn infants.

The Sickledex

Another test that has been used in large-scale testing programs is the Sickledex. A drop of blood is put in a test tube with several chemicals that cause the outer membranes of the red blood cells to burst, allowing their contents to leak out. (This process is called hemolysis; the main substance that leaks out is hemoglobin.) Normal hemoglobin dissolves readily in the solution in the test tube, but hemoglobin S is less soluble. So, if the fluid turns cloudy after a short time, this means sickle cells are present. If the fluid is clear, the blood is normal.

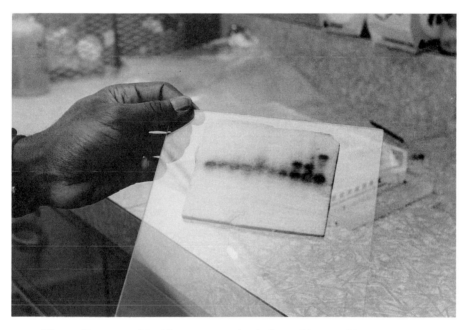

The sodium metabisulfite test can check for sickling in blood cells, as shown here.

Major disadvantages of the Sickledex test, like the sodium metabisulfite test, are that it cannot distinguish between sickle cell trait and sickle cell anemia, and it is unreliable for newborns. It can also be rather expensive.

The Dithionite Test

A variation of the Sickledex test is the automated dithionite test. This test uses the same chemicals as the Sickledex test, but everything is automated. Since the test tube readings are done by machine, the process is faster and less costly. But this test, like the Sickledex and the sodium metabisulfite test, cannot be used to screen newborn infants. Even babies with two sickle cell genes have too little Hb S in their blood to give a positive test. (During development before birth and for a while afterward, the blood contains mainly fetal hemoglobin, in which two alpha chains are combined with two gamma globin chains instead of two beta chains.)

The Technicon System

Another automated test is called the Technicon System. A drop of blood is put in a little cup mixed with a special chemical formula. The machine reads the solution by making a tracing on graph paper. If the person has sickle cell anemia or sickle cell trait, the line makes a big peak. If the test comes out positive, a second test can be done to indicate whether the person has sickle cell anemia or sickle cell trait. In the second test, the height of the peak of the line depends on how much

46

sickle hemoglobin there is. The peak observed for a person with sickle cell anemia will be twice as high as the peak for someone with sickle cell trait.

Electrophoresis Tests

Electrophoresis was the technique that was first used to discover the abnormal hemoglobin in the blood of people with sickle cell anemia, and variations of the test developed by Dr. Linus Pauling are still the most widely used today to diagnose the disease. This test is not only able to determine if a patient has sickle cell trait or sickle cell anemia; it can also indicate if the person has other related blood disorders, such as thalassemia, hemoglobin C, or hemoglobin D. To test for sickle cell disease, a sample of blood is treated in the laboratory to break down the cells and release their hemoglobin. The solution is then put on filter paper or a gel, and an electric current is applied. The hemoglobins are separated, according to their electrical charges, making it possible to identify which kind they are. Thus, sickle cell trait or sickle cell anemia can be determined. Electrophoresis testing used to be very time-consuming and expensive. However, improvements have made it quicker, simpler, less costly, and very reliable. (A typical test would cost the patient about $50. In cellulose acetate electrophoresis, two hundred samples can be tested per hour.)[2] Several tests, using variations of the basic technique, may be run to distinguish between different forms of hemoglobin.

Predicting and Preventing Strokes

Strokes are the most serious side effects among children with sickle cell disease. Studies have found that 8 to 17 percent of sickle cell patients have strokes, most often during childhood and adolescence. The result may be learning disabilities, paralysis, or even death.

An ultrasound device, called a transcranial Doppler imager, allows doctors to try to prevent strokes in children by identifying which children have the greatest risk. It has been found that changes occur in the brain blood vessels of many children with sickle cell disease. The arteries gradually narrow, making them more likely to be plugged up when blood cells sickle and pile up together. Such plugs could cut off the blood flow to parts of the brain, resulting in death of brain tissues— a stroke. The Doppler imager shows the narrowed areas that are potential trouble spots.

In a study of 250 children with sickle cell anemia, the Doppler imager was used to determine which ones had a good chance of suffering a stroke. The study revealed that forty of these children had narrowing arteries. Later, seven children in this study suffered strokes. All but one of the seven had been identified by the ultrasound device as being at risk for strokes.

If doctors are able to identify the children who are susceptible to strokes, they may be able to prevent them by giving monthly blood transfusions, which replace part of the red blood cells containing sickle hemoglobin with normal red cells—enough to keep the blood from sickling and to prevent dangerous blockage of the brain's blood vessels.[3]

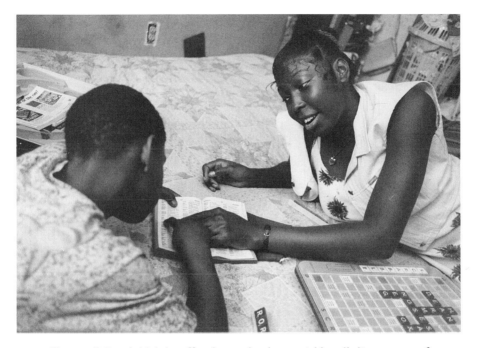

Shawntell Royal (right) suffered a stroke due to sickle cell disease, one of the disease's most serious side effects. She is shown here with her brother Terrance Royal.

A researcher at the National Heart, Lung, and Blood Institute is engaged in the study of sickle cell anemia. A new test, known as chorionic villus sampling, promises to advance the prenatal diagnosis of genetic blood diseases.

Prenatal Diagnosis

Sickle cell disease can actually be detected before birth. There are tests that can determine if the fetus will have sickle cell anemia, carry the trait, or be normal.

One test, called amniocentesis, can be done by collecting and testing the amniotic fluid that surrounds the unborn baby while it is still in the mother's body. This procedure can be performed during the sixteenth week of pregnancy when there is enough amniotic fluid. Amniocentesis can be used to test for a number of hereditary conditions in addition to sickle cell disease, but this process takes a long time to give results.

An alternative to amniocentesis for prenatal diagnosis is a method called chorionic villus sampling (CVS). A woman who is less than eleven weeks pregnant may use this type of testing. Chorionic villi are a part of the tissues that surround the fetus and eventually become the placenta, or afterbirth. A small sample of the chorionic villi is taken, containing enough fetal cells for immediate genetic analysis.

Getting a Second Opinion

No matter which test one chooses for diagnosing sickle cell disease, it is important to have the test done at least twice. The possibility of false positives and false negatives is very real. It can be a nightmare if a person tests positive and thinks he or she has the disease, when actually the test was wrong. Incorrectly testing negative may be an even greater nightmare.

5

Treatment

The normal blood cells that change from round to sickle varies
The pain starts when there's a lack of oxygen in the capillaries
A Crisis is described as a period of time
Dehydration or infection can trigger it again
When a crisis comes on, you hydrate and get rest
To find out if one has it is done with a simple blood test
The one thing about the disease that it doesn't discriminate
The only way to get it, both parents must have the trait
It is not acquired, but it is genetic
It won't get the best of you, unless you let it
Being sick all the time you create hospital bills
When the pain isn't so bad you can just take pills
When I feel a crisis coming on I know I'm doomed

That's when I go to the Emergency Room
I go receive treatment and hopefully I'm released
Until it flares up again I'm in perfect peace.
— From "Sickle Cell The Inside Story," poem by Karen
    Duggins (a person with sickle cell anemia)[1]

This poem is the perception of one person with sickle cell anemia. Many sickle cell sufferers would agree that it is a perfect description of their experiences with the disease. Sickle cell patients are often given painkillers or intravenous fluids for immediate relief. However, these methods do not always work, so doctors try a number of other treatments that may work for some people and not others.

Blood Transfusions

Blood transfusions are often a very effective way to relieve the pain caused by sickle cell disease. Some doctors give transfusions of whole blood. Others give transfusions of packed red cells. The use of only red-cell, rather than whole-blood, tranfusions does well in keeping the blood hemoglobin as normal as possible.

The job of blood transfusions is to increase the number of red blood cells, to maintain the level of normal red blood cells. This keeps the number of sickled cells below the critical point that may cause a pain episode. However, transfusions are not recommended as a routine way of relieving a person's pain episodes. Not only are they inconvenient, but there are some dangers in any blood transfusion. Although donor blood is carefully screened, there is a small possibility that it might contain hepatitis or even AIDS viruses; the recipient might also develop a reaction due to an imperfect match to all the proteins the donor blood contains. Transfusions should be used only in life-threatening situations, such as when there is a risk of a stroke or other complications.

Surgery is another situation when blood transfusions are commonly given. People with sickle cell disease may need surgery to repair damage caused by blood-vessel blockage— joint replacement, for example, as well as nose and throat operations to open blocked airways. Doctors routinely give such patients blood transfusions a few days before surgery in an effort to prevent complications due to poor oxygen supply to the tissues. It was believed that such patients should receive about five units of blood, enough to lower their sickle hemoglobin levels to 30 percent or less of the total hemoglobin. But a recent five-year study, conducted at thirty-six medical centers, found that sickle cell patients actually do better when they receive fewer transfusions before surgery—about 2.5 units, just enough to correct anemia. Dr. Oswaldo Castro, director of Howard University's Center for Sickle Cell Disease in Washington, D.C., notes that even less blood may be needed for patients who are using hydroxyurea therapy to help correct the sickle cell condition.[2]

Fetal Hemoglobin

In 1990, hydroxyurea, an experimental drug normally used to treat cancer, became the first sign of hope for treating the

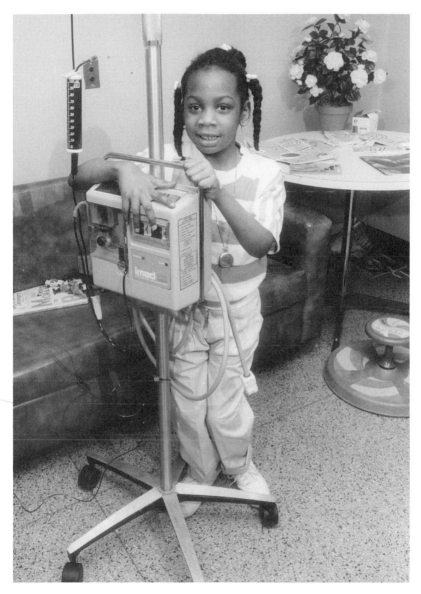

Annamnique Cressinger receives treatment for sickle cell disease.

underlying causes of the sickle cell disease rather than just the symptoms.

Hydroxyurea stimulates the production of fetal hemoglobin. (This, remember, is the special form of hemoglobin that is produced in the blood during fetal development and for about six months after birth.) A newborn infant has about 80 percent fetal hemoglobin, which contains two alpha chains combined with two gamma chains. Fetal hemoglobin molecules do not have the right chemical structure to join together and form polymer fibers. As Johns Hopkins researcher Dr. Samuel Charache describes it, "It's like children's building blocks with pegs and holes in them: You could make a big tall tower of them. That's just what happens with sickled hemoglobin: A whole string of them get stuck together." But fetal hemoglobin, with its gamma chains, "doesn't have the peg or the hole."[3] So, as long as there is plenty of this form of hemoglobin, the red blood cells are protected from sickling. But soon after birth, the special gene responsible for producing fetal hemoglobin is turned off. More of the beta chains are produced, and by one year of age, the amount of fetal hemoglobin has fallen to only 1 to 2 percent.

In the early 1970s, researchers studying people with sickle cell disease in Saudi Arabia and India discovered that many of them appeared perfectly healthy. They had never suffered from sickle cell episodes or anemia, even though they had inherited two sickle cell genes. Blood tests revealed that their bodies were producing much larger than normal amounts of fetal hemoglobin. This fetal protein actually carries more oxygen than the adult form of hemoglobin, so these people's fetal hemoglobin not only protected their blood cells from sickling but also did more than its share in supplying the body tissues with oxygen. These findings sparked a search for ways to turn the fetal hemoglobin gene back on in people with sickle cell disease.

Hydroxyurea was one of the drugs tested. In nationwide clinical trials with adults, it proved so dramatically effective that the researchers stopped the tests earlier than they had planned. Normally, when new drugs are tested, some of the people in the experiment serve as "controls": They are given only the usual treatment, or a placebo (that is, a harmless but inactive substance made up to look like the drug being tested). These controls provide a standard of comparison by which the effectiveness of the new drug can be judged. But the results with hydroxyurea were so good that it did not seem ethical to deny it to anyone who could benefit. People who took hydroxyurea each day had 50 percent fewer episodes than those who received the placebo, they needed only half as many blood transfusions, and they were hospitalized only half as often. Tests are now underway to determine whether the treatment is safe and effective for children.

Hydroxyurea has some disadvantages, though. It is toxic to bone marrow, where new blood cells are produced. It also can cause genetic mutations, and thus it should not be used by people planning to become parents. Recently researchers have tried combining hydroxyurea with erythropoietin, a growth hormone that stimulates red blood cell production. When combined with erythropoietin, a much smaller dose of hydroxyurea could be used, and the combination increased the amount of fetal hemoglobin more rapidly than even the highest dose of hydroxyurea alone. Using the combination is also a lot less harmful than using hydroxyurea alone.

Now researchers are developing other, less toxic drugs for increasing fetal hemoglobin production. One of them is based on a chemical found in our everyday foods—a food additive called butyrate. Butyrate is a simple fatty acid that is found in the body and is also used to enhance the flavor of food. Dr. Susan Perrine of Children's Hospital Oakland Research Institute in California began studying butyrate in the mid-1980s after reading a report that this substance turned on a gene in chickens that normally produces a blood protein in immature chicks. Working with a colleague at Boston University Medical School, Dr. Perrine found that high levels of butyrate in mothers with diabetes delayed the changeover from fetal to adult hemoglobin in their children. The next step was not as simple as feeding the food additive to people with sickle cell anemia, because butyrate eaten in foods turned out to have no effect on hemoglobin. Dr. Perrine prepared a compound, arginine butyrate, that could be injected into the bloodstream. In tests on patients with sickle cell anemia and beta-thalassemia, it produced substantial increases in fetal hemoglobin without any harmful effects. A newer drug form, isobutyramide, can be taken orally and is being developed by Vertex Pharmaceuticals of Cambridge, Massachusetts.[4]

Bone Marrow Transplants

Bone marrow transplants are another promising method of treatment for sickle cell patients. Bone marrow produces hemoglobin, and healthy bone marrow transplanted to a person with sickle cell anemia will theoretically produce healthy hemoglobin. However, because these transplants are risky and can cause serious complications, until recently they were performed only when the patient developed an additional life-threatening condition, such as leukemia.

In 1982, the University of Chicago Medical Center reported their first bone marrow transplant for sickle cell treatment. An eight-year-old girl, diagnosed with sickle cell anemia when she was two, developed leukemia and doctors decided to treat both of these conditions with a bone marrow transplant. The operation was successful, and after treatments to avoid transplant rejection, the young girl had no more pain episodes and remained in complete remission from leukemia. In addition, the level of hemoglobin S, the kind that produces sickle cells, fell from 78 percent before the transplant down to 20 percent afterwards. Hemoglobin A, the normal kind, was not detectable before the transplant but rose to 62 percent a month after the transplant. Subsequently, fifteen other sickle cell patients were treated with bone marrow transplants. Three of the fifteen also had a life-threatening illness. All fifteen survived the procedure.[5]

Gene Therapy

Another method that shows great promise in treating sickle cell anemia is called human gene therapy. It is still a new concept, so it is hard to theorize about the effects it may have on sickle cell disease. Researchers are very optimistic.

The purpose of gene therapy is to replace a defective gene with a normal one so that the genetic disease can ultimately be reversed. In gene therapy approaches to the treatment of sickle cell anemia, bone marrow cells (called stem cells) are removed from the patient. These cells are the ancestors of red blood cells. When their hemoglobin is corrected, their red-cell descendents can make the right kind of hemoglobin and prevent the blood from sickling.

In the laboratory, researchers transfer a normal hemoglobin gene to a virus called adeno-associated virus (AAV), related to a form of common cold virus. In culture dishes, the virus infects the patient's bone marrow cells. Viruses can transfer genes to the cells they infect. So some of the infected bone marrow cells pick up the normal hemoglobin gene. Red blood cells that are formed from these bone marrow cells will be able to make normal hemoglobin. The idea is to inject these bone marrow cells into the patient's bone marrow. Some bone marrow cells survive and multiply to produce normal red blood cells.

In the past, all doctors could do was treat the symptoms that resulted from hereditary defects. With gene therapy, they can repair the defects themselves. Some of the research on gene therapy will be described in Chapter 8.

6

Prevention

In the late 1960s, a group of African-American militants felt that the United States government was ignoring the sickle cell problem because of discrimination and racism. With the 1972 election year coming up, President Richard Nixon responded to their fears, requesting massive funding for sickle cell research and giving it national attention. This began the movement toward massive sickle cell screening.[1]

The First Screening Tests

In the early 1970s, the first sickle cell screening programs were started. Massachusetts became the first state (of thirteen) to pass a mandatory screening law. Unfortunately, many of these programs were poorly planned, with more input from politicians than from medical experts. Little attention was given to educating the community about the nature of the disease and what the tests meant. Well-meaning amateurs went around the neighborhoods with testing kits and left people with the knowledge that they were "carriers" but with little idea of what that meant or what to do about it.[2]

The purpose of the screening tests was supposed to be identifying those with sickle cell disease and those with the trait. However, being a carrier was often confused with having sickle cell disease. People were left with the impression that those with the trait were "sick," even though medical reports stated that sickle cell carriers do not have any increased health risks. By the late 1970s, many of the poorly planned programs were abandoned.

African Americans Became a Target

A total of thirty states conducted sickle cell screening programs. Since sickle cell disease affected mostly African Americans, they became the target group for these screening programs. However, health officials eventually realized that this target screening was incomplete and unfair. This type of screening was prejudicial and missed people with the disease who belong to other groups.

In the early 1990s, a National Institutes of Health panel recommended that all newborns be screened for sickle cell disease, regardless of their race. Even though sickle cell disease is most prevalent among African Americans, this blood disorder occurs in almost all racial and ethnic groups. Moreover, as the panel's report pointed out, it is not always easy to determine people's race or ethnic group accurately.[3] Skin color and other characteristics vary greatly. Going by typical African, Asian, or Hispanic names can also be misleading, since each includes a very diverse group of people from different parts of the world and people who acquired the names by marriage. Some of the target screening programs had been based on questionnaires where people identified their race; but these self-reports can sometimes be misleading. (Each individual, remember, has inherited traits from parents, grandparents, great-grandparents, and so on—often resulting in mixtures that are not very well described by the simple check-off boxes in a questionnaire.) So, if only African Americans are screened for sickle cell, there is a chance that others with the disease will be missed. In a study done in North Carolina, for example, it was found that target screening missed about 20 percent of the children with sickle cell disease.[4]

How Screening Works

Newborn screening is done shortly after birth by placing a drop of blood from the infant's heel on a piece of filter paper or taking a liquid sample from the umbilical cord. The liquid samples are more stable. (The spots on filter paper are good for only a week at room temperature.) Liquid samples also have the advantage that repeated or additional tests can be run from the same sample. A dried blood spot on filter paper (a Guthrie card) is very convenient because it can easily be incorporated into other newborn screening programs.

The sample is screened through electrophoresis testing. Screening has become highly specialized over the years. Computerized testing procedures can analyze a sample of blood or urine for hundreds of different components. Large groups of people can be tested for a variety of hereditary conditions for just a few dollars a person. So the screening includes not only sickle cell testing but also tests for other hemoglobin abnormalities such as hemoglobin C, hemoglobin E, and beta-thalassemia.

What Good Is Screening?

In the 1970s, people questioned why sickle cell screening was necessary. After all, there was (and still is) no cure. There was no way of preventing the disease. However, studies have shown that newborn screening has become essential in long-term survival. If a child's sickle cell status is identified at birth, daily doses of penicillin can be started immediately. Infection is the most common cause of death in children with sickle cell disease, and penicillin helps fight off the life-threatening infections before they develop.

Doctors recommend that penicillin be taken daily until the child is five or six years old, when the immune system is stronger. Fortunately, there seem to be no serious side effects, and the treatment really works. Studies have shown that babies given penicillin every day had 84 percent fewer infections—and none died.[5] Immunization against common diseases, especially pneumococcal pneumonia, also helps protect the child's health.

Preventing Episodes

Prevention is the key. Although the disease itself cannot be prevented, certain precautions can be taken to avoid symptoms or lessen the severity. First of all, a person with sickle cell anemia needs to eat properly. With a balanced diet, including meat, poultry, or fish, grains, dairy products, fruits, and vegetables, the body is better equipped to fight off any infections. Taking vitamins in addition to well-balanced meals is also very helpful. For instance, folic acid supplements help the body make more red blood cells. Folic acid (a B vitamin) can also be found in leafy vegetables, mushrooms, fruit, and liver.

Drinking plenty of fluids is equally important. It is a good idea to drink some water or juice every hour. This keeps the blood flowing well, which prevents the sickle cells in the blood vessels from clumping. When people with sickle cell anemia do not get enough fluids, they become weak, which can bring on a crisis.

People with sickle cell anemia tire easily, so it is very important that they get plenty of rest. If they get tired in the middle of the afternoon, they need to stop what they are doing and take a nap, even if only for a short time.

Sickle cell sufferers should exercise every day. It should not be too strenuous—just walking can help keep the body in shape and healthy enough to prevent illnesses. Overdoing it

Daily exercise is important for people with sickle cell disease. Here, Elizabeth Punter and her brother, Tasheem, get plenty of exercise on the school playground.

and exercising to the point of exhaustion is not a good idea, since stress can bring on an episode. Taking a rest now and then can help one keep from overexerting.

People with sickle cell anemia should avoid alcohol or drugs. They have been known to bring on pain episodes. Drugs and alcohol produce an acid condition when they are broken down in the body. This tends to make the blood cells sickle more. A doctor should be consulted before taking any medications.

Wintertime can be very difficult for sickle cell sufferers. One of the ways the body normally copes with cold is by constricting the blood vessels in the skin, to cut down the loss of body heat radiating from the blood flowing close to the surface. Yet the reduced blood flow means less oxygen in these tissues, and sickled cells may plug the narrowed vessels, bringing on a pain episode. So people with sickle cell disease need to dress as warmly as possible when it is cold outside.

People with sickle cell anemia should stay away from placcs where the oxygen is low, since oxygen deprivation can cause blood cells to sickle. It would not be a good idea to go scuba diving or hiking in the mountains. Flying in commercial airplanes is safe because they are completely pressurized, but flying in some military planes can be dangerous since they may not be pressurized.

Probably the most important guideline sickle cell patients should follow is to stay away from any kind of infection. Since their immune systems are so weak and vulnerable, even a simple cold may bring on a pain episode. Pneumonia is one of the most common complications and is reponsible for a large number of deaths of children with sickle cell anemia.

Genetic Counseling

Screening tests make it possible to prevent sickle cell disease in future generations. Through genetic counseling, people who know or suspect that they carry sickle cell genes can find out more about the disease and the chances that their children will inherit their defective genes. The counselor explores the aspects of the disease with the couple, provides them with information, and discusses options.

Genetic counseling usually involves a three-step process. First, the genetic counselor needs a detailed family medical history. The counselor needs to be informed of any disorders in family members, which can be checked by running blood tests or chromosome analyses with their cooperation. The second step involves estimating the risk. The counselor, through test results and any pertinent medical publications, tries to calculate the risks of passing on the disease to future generations. Communication is the next task for the genetic counselor, who must explain to the couple exactly what kind of genetic risks they face, what the odds are, and what options they can choose to avoid giving birth to a child with the sickle cell defect. If the couple decides to take the risks, the genetic counselor will inform the couple of the treatments, the costs, the emotional stress involved, and the prospects for success.

The genetic counselor also talks to the couple about other alternatives if they do not wish to take a chance that their

Through genetic counseling, people who know or suspect they carry the sickle cell genes can find out more about the disease.

future children will inherit the disease. Some options that are used mainly to help people with infertility problems may be of special interest to couples with genetic risks. For instance, adoption is one possibility. Carriers may also consider artificial insemination. Semen from a male donor is inserted into the female at her most fertile time of the month. However, artificial insemination may be risky since semen donors are not usually screened for genetic disorders.

7

Sickle Cell Disease and Society

n the tiny village of Orchemenos in Greece, scientists discovered there was a high occurrence of sickle cell anemia. They realized that through a program of genetic screening and counseling, they could help villagers avoid marriages between carriers of the sickle cell gene. Since most of the marriages in the village of Orchemenos were arranged, this plan seemed possible. The health status of the potential partners became a critical consideration in the arrangement of marriages.

Each villager had to be screened for both sickle cell anemia and sickle cell trait. The scientists then counseled them on the meaning of their test results. However, despite the scientists' efforts to educate the villagers, they absorbed only part of the message. People who carried the sickle cell trait were lumped together with those who had the disease. Society considered the carriers inferior to the rest of the population, and they became outcasts. The carriers, shunned by the "healthy" villagers, tended to marry each other—so no progress at all was made toward wiping out the disease. Instead of helping these villagers, the new knowledge of their sickle cell status had become just another way for them to classify one another. It had created a new and stigmatized social class.[1]

Although sickle cell genetic screening is beneficial and necessary, it has proven to be a serious problem socially, not only for the people in Orchemenos, Greece, but in the United States, too. The 1970s became a very productive decade, but also a devastating one, for people with sickle cell disease.

The First National Program Passed

In 1972, Congress finally passed the National Sickle Cell Anemia Control Act.[2] This law established the first national program that provided funding to fight sickle cell disease through comprehensive research and sickle cell education for the public. Although this was a huge step in aiding people with sickle cell anemia, public awareness of this disease actually started to hurt their livelihood instead of helping it.

Target for Discrimination

For years, blacks have been trying to demonstrate that they are not inferior to whites. Just when African Americans started to gain equal rights, their old fears resurfaced as new knowledge of sickle cell disease came to the public. It became known that sickle cell disease occured mostly among African Americans. Many blacks believed this would give the white community an additional excuse to discriminate against them.[3]

Although it seemed as though African Americans were being singled out, society actually was becoming prejudiced against people with sickle cell disease. Fears of those with the disease prompted lawmakers to place special regulations and restrictions on people with sickle cell disease for the "protection" of society as a whole. Every aspect of their lives was affected. They became a target of discrimination.

Sickle Cell Disease in School

Children with the sickle cell disease faced discrimination in schools. The prejudices came from ignorance. Parents in school were afraid that their child would catch this illness. Other children were prompted to keep their distance from the sickle cell sufferer, which could lead to serious emotional scars. Education is a very important tool that should be used to teach people the facts about sickle cell disease, especially that sickle cell disease is not contagious.

Another problem in schools is that school personnel may worry that a child with sickle cell disease will be too much of a burden. Teachers need to be fully informed of the child's problem and what to do in case of an emergency. They may feel an overwhelming sense of responsibility in being asked to take care of a very sick child. So laws were passed, restricting the

73

access of children with sickle cell disease to school facilities. In the early 1970s, for example, children had to be screened for the sickle cell trait before they were allowed to attend a public school in Massachusetts.[4]

Sickle Cell Screening Before Marriage

In the early 1970s, New York passed a law stating that African Americans had to be screened for sickle cell trait before applying for a marriage license.[5] The lawmakers were concerned that carriers would pass the trait on to their children. If they did have the sickle cell trait, they had to seek genetic counseling. They were then advised not to have children so that their offspring would not develop the disease.

Carrier screening programs, however, were generally a failure in reducing the number of children born to people with the sickle cell trait. They were insensitive to the social and psychological dynamics of the communities and families involved.[6] Low income, teenage pregnancies, and out-of-wedlock births are more prevalent among African Americans than in the rest of the population. Meaningful communication and long-range family planning are rare for couples who grew up in such circumstances. Moreover, having children has traditionally been an important human goal. Denying this goal would require far more motivation than vaguely understood probabilities that a child with a disabling illness might be born. Even women who are already coping with the burden of caring for a child with sickle cell anemia often choose to have more children. One mother, who considered herself "lucky" because only two of

Choosing whether or not to have a child is an important decision for parents who carry the sickle cell trait.

her four children had sickle cell disease, commented about her state of mind before the birth of the fourth child: "I thought about it, but not too much. 'Cause they told me that it was chance that other kids might have it, but only one had it. The other kids didn't have it."[7] The willingness of other family members, such as grandmothers or aunts, to help out with the burdens of child care may also contribute to the low degree of concern about having a child with the disease.

Sickle Cell Disease in the Workplace

As awareness of sickle cell anemia grew, discrimination became more widespread. People even tried to keep their sickle cell illness a secret from their employers because they believed their job would no longer be secure. A boss might think that the sufferer could no longer handle the job or that the job might pose a threat to the person's well-being. Frequent hospitalizations for sickle cell episodes could get a person fired.

Another important area of discrimination was the refusal of insurance companies to write health and life insurance policies for people with sickle cell disease.[8] Insurance also affects jobs. Many employers provide group policies—but if the group includes people likely to have heavy medical expenses, the insurance rates may go up. So hiring people with sickle cell anemia could be risky for an employer.

Sickle Cell Disease in the Military

In 1968 and 1969, four army recruits who had the sickle cell trait died during intense basic training at Fort Bliss. It was reported that the recruits died because their blood cells sickled during strenuous exercise at high altitude. An autopsy revealed that all of the victims had severely sickled red blood cells. This report led to the banning of sickle cell carriers in the Army.

In 1973, an Air Force doctor reported that two African-American Air Force Academy cadets died during an intense training exercise that happened to be at a high altitude. After studying all available information, the National Academy of Sciences requested that African Americans with sickle cell trait be banned from being pilots or copilots.

However, in 1980, a survey was conducted by retired Air Force flight surgeon Vance A. Marchbanks on 154 African-American pilots who had served during and after World War II. He reported that ten of these pilots had the sickle cell trait, and none of them had any problems in flight even in unpressurized planes where the oxygen levels were low.

In February 1981, researchers realized that the 1973 report needed to be reevaluated. They discovered that both of the Air Force Academy cadets who had collapsed and died had been recovering from influenza. They revealed that the red blood cells of patients with sickle cell trait start to sickle after death. This showed that the autopsies done on those army recruits at Fort Bliss did not prove that sickle cell trait caused their deaths. That same year, the Air Force Academy dropped its ban on accepting people with the sickle cell trait.[9]

The final chapter of this story may not have been written, however. A United States Army study of unexplained deaths during strenuous basic training reported in 1987 that

African-American recruits with sickle cell trait had a risk of sudden exercise-related death that was twenty-eight times higher than for African-American recruits without the trait and forty times higher than for all other recruits. "This is the first compelling evidence that sickle cell trait is related to disease," commented Dr. John A. Kark of the Walter Reed Army Institute of Research and the Armed Forces Institute of Pathology. To put those scary-sounding numbers in perspective, the actual risk of death for the recruits with sickle cell trait was 1 in 3,200. Dr. Kark also points out that the researchers had found only a statistical connection between the trait and the deaths, not an explanation for why the deaths occurred or any indication of how much exercise was responsible.[10]

Sickle Cell Disease and the Future

8

R esearch on sickle cell disease has made great strides
since its discovery. In the past, people with sickle cell
anemia rarely lived past twenty years old. Now, with
new treatments, they can live into their fifties and sixties. As
recently as the mid-1980s, 20 percent of children with sickle
cell disease died before they reached the age of three; now,
with widespread screening programs and daily penicillin treatments to help fight infections, less than 3 percent of these
children die.[1]

Treatments for sickle cell anemia have always been targeted
at the symptoms instead of the disease itself—until now.
Scientists are very enthusiastic about the wave of the future:
human gene therapy.

A Bold Gamble That Backfired

Martin Cline, a specialist in blood disorders at the University of California in Los Angeles, made one of the first attempts at gene therapy. During the 1970s, he had done pioneering work on bone marrow transplants and chemotherapy for leukemia and lymphoma (a bone marrow cancer). By 1976, he was convinced that the future of medicine lay in manipulating genes at the molecular level. Teaming up with Winston Salser, a UCLA colleague who specialized in genetic engineering, Dr. Cline quickly learned the basic techniques for introducing bits of DNA (the chemical of heredity) into cells. At first he focused on trying to identify the genes involved in leukemia. Then it occurred to him that the techniques he was developing could also be used to insert normal hemoglobin genes into the cells of people with sickle cell anemia or beta-thalassemia. The beta globin gene had recently been isolated by Dr. Thomas Maniatis at Cal Tech. So all the needed elements appeared to be in place.

Dr. Cline did his preliminary experiments with mice. First he set out to use gene transfer techniques to make mice resistant to the anticancer drug methotrexate. This drug kills cancer cells by preventing them from utilizing a vitamin, folic acid, but it is also rather toxic to normal cells and can cause severe destruction of a cancer patient's bone marrow. If the normal marrow cells could be made resistant to methotrexate, then larger doses of the drug could be given to wipe out the cancer cells more effectively. Cline attempted to do this by introducing extra copies of the gene for a key enzyme of folic

ERRORS IN THE CODE

The instructions contained in our genes are spelled out in a biochemical called DNA (deoxyribonucleic acid). Like proteins, DNA molecules are polymers—long chains composed of chemical building blocks. The building blocks of proteins are amino acids, of which there are about twenty kinds; those of DNA are called nitrogen bases, and they come in four main varieties: adenine (A), cytosine (C), guanine (G), and thymine (T). It seems incredible that the complicated information for making and operating a human being could all be spelled out in a four-letter alphabet—but remember, all the words in the English language can be spelled out in Morse code, which has only two letters (dot and dash). The DNA bases are also a code, which translates the amino acids in proteins. Each three letters in DNA correspond to one amino acid in the protein formed from the gene's blueprints. For example, GAG in a gene would be translated into the amino acid glutamate in a protein. The error that substitutes a different amino acid, valine, for glutamate in the sixth position on the beta globin chain, producing Hb S, is the result of a mistake in just one letter in the DNA alphabet: GTG instead of GAG. Other errors in different parts of the beta globin gene result in other types of blood disorders, such as beta-thalassemia.

acid metabolism into mouse bone marrow cells. More than one-third of the treated mice did become methotrexate-resistant.

Other researchers were unable to repeat Dr. Cline's experiments, and they believed that he had not demonstrated that gene transfer had actually occurred. After another series of experiments, in which Dr. Cline transferred a different gene to mouse cells, he submitted an application to his university review board to transfer normal hemoglobin genes to patients with sickle cell anemia. Meanwhile, he had similar applications pending at hospitals in Israel and Italy for the treatment of thalassemia. Later, many researchers objected to this "premature" attempt to treat humans, when the animal experiments had not yet been fully proven. (Dr. Cline's attempts to get the human hemoglobin gene to work in mice had failed.) Dr. Cline believed that his proposal was justified. He said:

> The mouse experiments had gone on for two years and we had done several hundred animals, with no observed toxic side effects. . . . I envisioned that it would probably take at least a decade to perfect gene therapy techniques in humans, but I thought it appropriate to try the equivalent of a phase one study [that is, to find out whether there were any harmful effects and determine the best dose for humans]. We also wished to determine whether, in fact, the genes got in.[2]

The board members at UCLA refused Dr. Cline's application, complaining that more animal studies were needed before he could experiment on people. However, his applications at the foreign hospitals were granted. Cline treated bone marrow cells from a young woman in Jerusalem with beta-hemoglobin genes, together with viral genes that Cline thought would give the transformed marrow cells a survival edge over the untransformed cells. Cline injected about 500 million treated marrow cells, perhaps five thousand to fifty thousand of which might have been expected to have picked up the new genes. A few days later, Cline administered a similar treatment to a young thalassemia patient in Naples. However, neither experiment appeared to work. There was no sign that either of the thalassemia patients produced normal beta hemoglobin after the treatment.

Soon word about the gene transfer leaked out and shocked the medical community. Dr. Thomas Maniatis, who had supplied the beta globin gene, complained that he had no idea Dr. Cline intended to use it on humans. Dr. Richard Axel, whose research team had developed the gene transfer technique, stated, "There is simply no scientific basis for expecting this experiment to work in people."[3] Dr. Eliezer Rachmilewitz of Hadassah Hospital in Jerusalem had a different view. "I'm a doctor who is trying to do the best I can for my patient," he said. "This girl is at the end of the line. This is her only hope."[4] And Dr. Cline protested that the desperate condition of the patients justified desperate measures. It would take years for gene transfer techniques to be fully worked out in the laboratory—and by that time, it would be too late for these patients.

The National Institutes of Health did not agree and found Dr. Cline guilty of violating federal guidelines for human experiments. This turned out to be the biggest mistake of his career. The funding for Dr. Cline's research was cut back drastically, and his further research projects were hampered by frustrating red tape.

Progress in Gene Therapy

Although the early attempts were unsuccessful, other scientists learned from Cline's misfortune and proceeded more cautiously. In 1988, a British research team reported the successful transfer to adult mice of the human gene that directs beta-hemoglobin production. Not only were the transplanted genes functioning successfully in some of the mice nine months later, but they were functioning only in the appropriate kinds of cells—red blood cells and the bone marrow cells that produce them.

Bone marrow cells have thus far been the main target of gene therapy experiments because they can be fairly easily removed from the body and later replaced; they also have the potential to multiply rapidly and produce large quantities of their genetically engineered product. For blood disorders such as sickle cell anemia, bone marrow is a particularly appropriate target, since the blood-forming cells can be treated directly.

Most experiments in gene therapy are done ex vivo, or outside the body. Ex vivo techniques involve the removal of blood or tissue samples from a patient. The appropriate cells—for example, bone marrow stem cells—are separated from the material, treated to introduce corrected genes, and then returned to the patient's body. This is the only method that has proven to be effective so far. It has been used successfully to treat children born with deficiencies of the immune system that made them unable to fight disease germs. One of these hereditary immune deficiencies, ADA, was first successfully treated in 1990. Two young girls, lacking a key enzyme needed for the functioning of the body's defenses against disease, were given ex vivo treatments that introduced the gene for the missing enzyme. The girls lead relatively healthy lives now. In May 1995, researchers at Children's Hospital in Los Angeles reported that infants with ADA, treated by gene therapy, were now producing the needed enzyme on their own.[5]

Ex vivo treatment is fine for now, but the ultimate goal is in vivo treatment, in which corrective genes can be injected directly into a person's bloodstream. Some researchers are developing specially modified viruses to carry the genes and deliver them to the appropriate cells. Others are injecting bits of "naked DNA," either by itself or enclosed in fatty molecules called lipids. In still other futuristic experiments, researchers are using delicate surgical tools to inject DNA into egg cells, attempting to correct hereditary defects in future generations.

Meanwhile, research on sickle cell anemia was given a big boost in 1990, when scientists at the National Institute for Medical Research in London, England, announced the creation of "sickler mice." By inserting the human sickle cell gene into mouse embryos, they obtained a strain of mice whose red blood cells sickled under low-oxygen conditions.

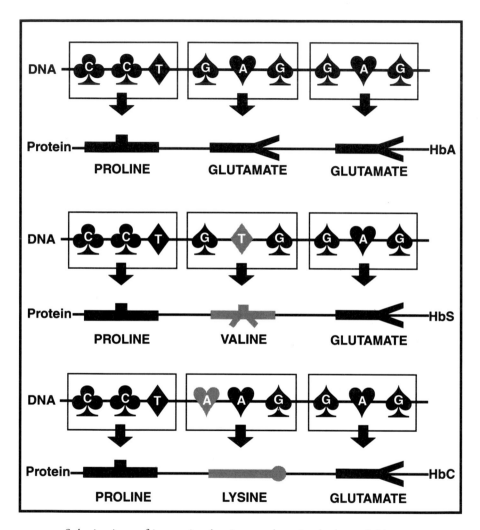

Substitutions of just a simple nitrogen base in the beta-globin gene can result in abnormal hemoglobin. Replacement of A by T leads to HbS, with the amino acid valine in place of a glutamate in the normal HbA. Substitution of A for G in the "code" for the same glutamate results in its replacement by lysine, in HbC.

Although the mice did not develop anemia (they were more like people with sickle cell trait), this was the first step toward an animal model of sickle cell disease, on which drugs and other treatments could be tested.

New Ethical Dilemmas

The results of a five-year international study, reported in 1996, showed that in some cases bone marrow transplants can cure sickle cell anemia but it also carries risks of infertility and even death. Doctors and patients are now faced with a dilemma: Is the chance of a cure worth a 10 percent or higher risk for dying, when current treatments allow people with sickle cell anemia to live for decades? Dr. Keith Sullivan, the leader of the study, believes that bone marrow transplants might best be used for patients in danger of stroke and those already suffering from complications.[6]

Although the blood-producing stem cells are found mainly in the bone marrow in adults, during the early months of development before birth, most red blood cells are produced in the liver. This organ (the largest organ in the body) is a lot easier to get to than bone marrow. So it might be possible to treat people with sickle cell disease by transplanting bits of fetal liver. In fact, the best time for such treatments might be before birth. (After the immune system is fully developed, potentially dangerous transplant rejection may occur unless the transplanted tissue is a nearly perfect match, biochemically, to the recipient's own cells. But the immune system of a fetus does not attack foreign tissues. Likewise, the fetal tissue in the transplant does not attack the recipient's body; so there is no danger of the kind of "graft versus host reaction" that can sometimes lead to death after a bone marrow transplant.) In 1994, researchers in France reported that they had successfully treated a fetus with Hurler's syndrome (a rare and very serious developmental disorder) with fetal tissue transplants. The child was born healthy and showed no signs of hereditary disease.

The question of using fetal tissue for transplants, however, has generated a great controversy. The main problem is that most fetal tissue is obtained after abortions, to which many people are opposed. They claim that the use of fetal tissue for "good" purposes might be used to justify abortions—or even to prompt the conception of children who would then be aborted and cut up for "spare parts." Researchers hope to get around these objections by developing techniques to grow fetal tissue in culture or, even better, to isolate the unique substances in fetal tissue that allow it to be freely transplanted and incorporate them into laboratory tissue cultures.

However these dilemmas are resolved, sickle cell anemia is now the focus of intense research efforts, and these efforts appear destined to bring effective new treatments and, ultimately, real cures. As Dr. Samuel Charache of Johns Hopkins University School of Medicine remarked in connection with the successful trials of hydroxyurea, "The most important part of it all is that patients know that this is concrete evidence that scientists have been doing things [to make progress against the disease]. That's the ray of hope, I think."[7]

Q & A

Q. Somebody in my class has sickle cell disease. Can I catch it if I borrow his notebook?

A. No. You can't "catch" sickle cell disease. It's not carried by a germ. It is a hereditary disease. The only way you can get it is by inheriting the genes for it from your parents.

Q. My little sister just got diagnosed with sickle cell anemia. Does that mean I have it, too?

A. Not necessarily—and if you haven't had any symptoms by now, it's likely that you don't have the disease. But there's a good chance that you do have sickle cell trait, so it would be a good idea to have a blood test.

Q. If I have sickle cell trait, does that mean I'm sick?

A. No. Most people with sickle cell trait never have any health problems related to it, but there may be some risk for you if you go mountain climbing or fly in an unpressurized airplane.

Q. So why do I need to find out if I have the trait?

A. If you have a sickle cell gene (the trait), you are likely to pass it to half of any children you may have. And if you marry someone who is also carrying the trait, your children will have a one in four chance of having sickle cell disease.

Q. You mean I should ask people whether they have the trait before I go out on a date with them?

A. Not necessarily, but it is something you need to know when you're making plans for marriage and a family. If you fall in love with someone who has sickle cell trait, it's your own personal decision whether to get married and even whether to take the chance of having children—but it's a decision you shouldn't make without knowing the facts.

Q. Is it sickle cell disease or sickle cell anemia?

A. Both terms are used. It is a hereditary disease (or disorder) that can lead to anemia (a shortage of oxygen-carrying red blood cells) because the sickle cells wear out faster than the bone marrow can replace them.

Q. What are the symptoms of sickle cell anemia?

A. The main symptoms are tiredness (because the energy-producing reactions in the body require oxygen, and blood containing sickle cells does not supply enough oxygen); slow growth; pains in the joints; swollen, painful hands and feet; an enlarged spleen; and periodic episodes of intense pain.

Q. What causes the episodes?

A. In many cases, this is not known. Episodes may be brought on when the body is under stress. The particular kind of stress may vary from one person to another, but very hot or very cold weather are common triggers.

Q. When we found out my little sister has sickle cell disease, the doctor said she has to take penicillin every day, even when she isn't sick. Is that good for her?

A. Yes, it may even save her life! Children with sickle cell anemia are very susceptible to infections, especially pneumonia. Some have even died within six hours after they first ran a fever. Penicillin helps the body fight germs before they have a chance to multiply and cause illness.

Q. What else can a person with sickle cell do to stay healthy?

A. Mainly the same things that are good for everybody—eat a well-balanced diet, drink plenty of fluids, get enough rest, and exercise regularly.

Sickle Cell Disease Timeline

1910—Dr. James B. Herrick published the first medical report on sickle cell anemia.

1926—Dr. Thomas P. Cooley and Dr. P. Lee described two forms of sickle cell disease: sickle cell anemia and sickle cell trait.

1945—Dr. Linus Pauling discovered that an abnormal form of hemoglobin was responsible for the sickling in sickle cell patients.

1956—Dr. Vernon Ingram made a distinction between normal and abnormal hemoglobin.

1972—Congress passed the National Sickle Cell Anemia Control Act. This law established the first national program that provided funding to fight sickle cell anemia.

1980—Dr. Martin Cline attempted a transfer of normal beta globin genes to two patients with beta-thalassemia.

1982—The University of Chicago Medical Center reported its first bone marrow transplant for sickle cell treatment.

1988—A British research team reported the successful transfer to adult mice of the human gene that directs beta-hemoglobin production.

1990—A cancer drug, hydroxyurea, was found to stimulate fetal hemoglobin production, preventing effects of sickle cell disease.

1993—A National Institutes of Health panel recommended universal newborn screening for sickle cell disease.

For More Information

Sickle Cell Disease

American Sickle Cell
Anemia Association
10300 Carnegie Ave.
Cleveland, OH 44106
(216) 229-8600

California State Department
of Health
Children's Medical Services
Branch
Sacramento, CA 95814

Cincinnati Comprehensive
Sickle Cell Center
Children's Hospital Medical
Center
Elland and Bethesda Aves.
Cincinnati, OH 45229

Clinical Center
Communications
9000 Rockville Pike
Building 10, Room 1C255
Bethesda, MD 20892

Comprehensive Sickle Cell
Center
Boston City Hospital
818 Harrison Ave., FGH-2
Boston, MA 02118

Comprehensive Sickle Cell
Center
University of California
San Francisco General
Hospital
1001 Potrero Ave., Room 6J-5
San Francisco, CA 94110

Comprehensive Sickle Cell
Center
The Children's Hospital of
Philadelphia
34th St. & Civic Center
Blvd.
Philadelphia, PA 19104

Comprehensive Sickle Cell
Center
Meharry Medical College
Department of Pediatrics
1005 D. B. Todd, Jr., Blvd.
Nashville, TN 37208

Comprehensive Sickle Cell
Center
College of Physicians &
Surgeons
Columbia University
630 W. 168th St.
New York, NY 10032

Comprehensive Sickle Cell
Center
Duke University Medical
Center
Box 3934 Morris Building
Durham, NC 27710

Comprehensive Sickle Cell
Center
University of Southern
California
Department of Medicine
RMR 304
Los Angeles, CA 90033

Comprehensive Sickle Cell
Center
University of South
Alabama
College of Medicine
2451 Fillingim St.
Mobile, AL 36617

Comprehensive Sickle Cell
Center
Montefiore Hospital
Medical Center—
Rosenthal Main
111 E. 210th St.
Bronx, NY 10467

Education Programs
Associates
1 West Campbell Ave.,
Bldg. D
Campbell, CA 95008

Howard University
Comprehensive Sickle Cell
Center
2121 Georgia Ave., N.W.
Washington, DC 20059

March of Dimes
Birth Defects Foundation
1275 Mamaroneck Ave.
White Plains, NY 10605
(800) 367-6630
(Or look in the telephone
book for a local
March of Dimes chapter in
your area)

Mid-South Sickle Cell
Center
Le Bonheur Children's
Medical Center
Memphis, TN 38103

National Maternal and
Child Health
Clearinghouse
8201 Greensboro Dr., Suite
600
McLean, VA 22102

Mississippi State
Department of Health
Genetics Division
P.O. Box 1700
Jackson, MS 39215

New York State
Department of Health
Newborn Screening Program
Wadsworth Center for
Laboratories and Research
P.O. Box 509
Albany, NY 12201-0509

National Association for
Sickle Cell Disease
3345 Wilshire Blvd., Suite
1106
Los Angeles, CA
90010-1880
(800) 421-8453

Sickle Cell Disease
Association of America
200 Corporate Point,
Suite 495
Culver City, CA 90230
(800) 421-8453

National Institutes of
Health Sickle Cell Disease
Scientific Research Group
NHLBI, NIH
6701 Rockledge Drive,
MSC-7950
Bethesda, MD 20892
(301) 435-0055

Sickle Cell Disease Branch
NHLBI
National Institutes of
Health
7550 Wisconsin Ave.,
Room 508
Bethesda, MD 20892

Texas Department of
Health
Newborn Screening
Program
1100 W. 49th St.
Austin, TX 78756-7111

Triad Sickle Cell Anemia
Foundation
1102 East Market St.
Greensboro, NC 27420
(919) 274-1507

Thalassemia (Cooley's Anemia)

AHEPA Cooley's Anemia
Foundation, Inc.
1909 Q Street, NW,
Suite 500
Washington, DC 20009
(202) 232-6300

Cooley's Anemia
Foundation, Inc.
129-09 26th Ave.,
Suite 203,
Flushing, NY 11354
(800) 522-7222

Chapter Notes

Chapter 1

1. Richard Levine, "Jesse Jackson: Heir to Dr. King?" *Harper Magazine,* March 1969, p. 58; John Pekkanen, "Black Hope, White Hope: The Jesse Jackson Style, Militant but Nonviolent," *Life,* November 21, 1969, pp. 67–76; James Haskins, *I Am Somebody!: A Biography of Jesse Jackson* (Hillside, N.J.: Enslow Publishers, 1992), pp. 61–62.

2. Associated Press, "Study Finds Life Span of Sickle Cell Anemia Patients Improving," *The Courier-News* (Bridgewater, N.J.), June 9, 1994, p. A-7.

Chapter 2

1. Shirley Motter Linde, *Sickle Cell: A Complete Guide to Prevention and Treatment* (New York: Pavilion Publishing Company, 1972), pp. 13–14.

2. Ibid., p. 15.

3. Linde, p. 15.

4. Ibid., p. 27.

5. Warren E. Leary, "Intractable Pain of Sickle Cell Begins to Yield," *The New York Times,* June 7, 1994, p. C3.

6. George Beshore, *Sickle Cell Anemia* (New York: Franklin Watts, 1994), p. 12.

7. Ibid., p. 55.

8. Beshore, pp. 15, 17.

9. Linde, p. 56.

Chapter 3

1. Joan Whitlow, "Despite Gains, Sickle Cell Still Kills," *Star-Ledger* (Newark, N.J.), October 3, 1993, sec. 6, pp. 1–2.

2. Ibid., p. 1.

3. Perri Klass, M.D., "A Familiar Patient: With Sickle Cell Disease, There Are Many Hidden Dangers," *American Health*, April 1993, pp. 86–88.

4. *Sickle Cell Disease: Screening, Diagnosis, Management, and Counseling in Newborns and Infants,* Public Health Service, National Institutes of Health, Clinical Practice Guideline No. 6, Rockville, Md., 1993, p. 1.

5. Jared Diamond, "Blood, Genes, and Malaria," *Natural History,* February 1989, p. 10.

6. Shirley A. Hill, *Managing Sickle Cell Disease in Low-Income Families* (Philadelphia: Temple University Press, 1994), p. 60.

7. Stephanie Whyche, "Sickle Cell Anemia Attacks 1 in 600 American Blacks," *The Courier-News* (Bridgewater, N.J.), December 18, 1988, p. B-6.

8. Warren E. Leary, "Intractable Pain of Sickle Cell Begins to Yield," *The New York Times,* June 7, 1994, p. C3.

9. Ibid.

10. Diamond, p. 18.

11. Ibid., p. 16; Randolph M. Nesse and George C. Williams, *Why We Get Sick* (New York: Random House, 1994), p. 99.

Chapter 4

1. Joan Whitlow, "Sickle Cell Patients Get Better Care But No Cure," *Star-Ledger* (Newark, N.J.), May 5, 1985, sec. 1, p. 81.

2. *Sickle Cell Disease: Screening, Diagnosis, Management, and Counseling in Newborns and Infants,* Public Health Service, National Institutes of Health, Clinical Practice Guideline No. 6, Rockville, Md., 1993, p. 22.

3. "Device Is Said to Help Predict Strokes in Sickle Cell Children," *The New York Times,* January 17, 1991, p. B7; Warren E. Leary, "Childhood Stroke: A Hidden Peril More Common Than Most Think," *The New York Times*, May 17, 1995, p. C11.

Chapter 5

1. *The Challenge,* (quarterly magazine of Howard University Center for Sickle Cell Disease), Summer 1994, p. 4.

2. Warren E. Leary, "Fewer Transfusions Urged for Sickle Cell Patients," *The New York Times,* August 2, 1995, p. C9.

3. Diane E. Loupe, "Breaking the Sickle Cycle," *Science News,* December 2, 1989, pp. 360–361.

4. Warren E. Leary, "Tests Offer First Hope for Treating Cause of Sickle Cell Disease," *The New York Times,* January 14, 1993, p. D25; "An Embryonic Answer," *The Economist,* February 4, 1995, p. 74.

5. George Beshore, *Sickle Cell Anemia* (New York: Franklin Watts, 1994), pp. 75–76.

Chapter 6

1. Zsolt Harsanyi and Richard Hutton, *Genetic Prophecy: Beyond the Double Helix* (New York: Rawson, Wade Publishers, 1981), p. 250.

2. Ibid.; Yvonne Baskin, *The Gene Doctors: Medical Genetics at the Frontier* (New York: William Morrow and Company, 1984), p. 129.

3. *Sickle Cell Disease: Screening, Diagnosis, Management, and Counseling in Newborns and Infants,* Public Health Service, National Institutes of Health, Clinical Practice Guideline No. 6, Rockville, Md., 1993, pp. 11–12.

4. Warren E. Leary, "Screening of All Newborns Urged for Sickle Cell Disease," *The New York Times,* April 28, 1993, p. C11.

5. *Sickle Cell Anemia,* Public Health Service, National Institutes of Health, 1990, p. 13.

Chapter 7

1. Zsolt Harsanyi and Richard Hutton, *Genetic Prophecy: Beyond the Double Helix* (New York: Rawson, Wade Publishers, 1981), pp. 243–245.

2. Shirley A. Hill, *Managing Sickle Cell Disease in Low-Income Families* (Philadelphia: Temple University Press, 1994), p. 15.

3. Harsanyi and Hutton, p. 250.

4. Ricki Lewis, "Genetic Screening—Fetal Signposts on a Journey of Discovery," *FDA Consumer,* December 1990, p. 17.

5. Ibid.

6. Hill, pp. 27–49.

7. Ibid., p. 87.

8. Lewis, p. 17.

9. George Beshore, *Sickle Cell Anemia* (New York: Franklin Watts, 1994), pp. 66–69.

10. *Los Angeles Times,* "Study Links Sickle Cell to Deaths of Black Soldiers," *The Courier-News* (Bridgewater, N.J.), September 24, 1987, p. A-6.

Chapter 8

1. Warren E. Leary, "Screening of All Newborns Urged for Sickle Cell Disease," *The New York Times,* April 28, 1993, p. C11.

2. Jeff Lyon and Peter Gorner, *Altered Fates: Gene Therapy and the Retooling of Human Life* (New York: W. W. Norton & Company, 1995), p. 70.

3. Yvonne Baskin, *The Gene Doctors: Medical Genetics at the Frontier* (New York: William Morrow and Company, 1984), p. 173.

4. Ibid., p. 174.

5. Lawrence M. Fisher, "Bottling the Stuff of Dreams," *The New York Times,* June 1, 1995, p. D6.

6. Warren E. Leary, "Some Cured of Sickle Cell Disease by Transplants of Bone Marrow," *The New York Times,* August 8, 1996, pp. A1, D21.

7. Marty Munson and Rosemary Iconis, "Head Off Crises: Drug May Prevent Sickle Cell Flare-Ups," *Prevention,* June 1995, p. 50.

Glossary

adeno-associated virus (AAV)—A form of cold virus that is being used in some gene therapy experiments to carry genes into the body.

alpha globin—One of the types of protein in the hemoglobin molecule.

amino acids—The chemical building blocks of proteins.

amniocentesis—A procedure used in prenatal diagnosis by collecting and testing fetal cells from the amniotic fluid that surrounds the fetus in its mother's womb.

anemia—A blood disorder in which the number of red blood cells (or the amount of hemoglobin) is below normal and insufficient to provide for the body's oxygen needs.

beta globin—One of the types of protein in the hemoglobin molecule. Most of the hereditary blood disorders, such as sickle cell disease and beta-thalassemia, are due to mutations in the beta globin chains.

bone marrow—A substance inside the cavities of bones that contains blood-forming cells.

butyrate—A food additive (flavor enhancer) that has been found to stimulate increased production of fetal hemoglobin.

chorionic villus sampling (CVS)—Procedure used in prenatal diagnosis by testing samples from the placenta tissues surrounding the early fetus.

chromosomes—Structures inside the nucleus of each cell that contain the genes, coded in the form of DNA.

dithionite test—A test that detects sickle hemoglobin.

DNA (deoxyribonucleic acid)—The chemical of heredity, containing coded instructions for making body proteins.

dominant trait—A hereditary characteristic that is expressed even if the person has inherited the gene for it from only one parent.

Doppler imager—An ultrasound device used to detect narrowed blood vessels that present a danger of stroke.

electrophoresis—A technique for separating closely related chemicals according to their movement on a gel-coated slide or other surface in an electric field. The movement depends on the amount and distribution of electrical charges each molecule contains.

erythrocyte—A red blood cell.

fetal hemoglobin—The main form of hemoglobin in the blood before birth and for a short time after birth.

folic acid—A B vitamin needed for the production of red blood cells.

gamma globin—A protein found in fetal hemoglobin in place of the beta chains.

gene therapy—The transfer of normal (or genetically engineered) genes to correct a hereditary disorder.

genes—The units of heredity. Each gene contains the instructions for making a protein.

genetic counseling—A program of testing, compiling of family histories, and determination of potential risks to help a couple make family planning decisions.

hand-foot syndrome—Painful redness and swelling of the hands and feet in children with sickle cell anemia.

hemoglobin—A red pigment in red blood cells that carries oxygen or carbon dioxide. Its molecule is made up of protein chains (globins) and a central iron-containing substance (heme). Hb A is the normal form of hemoglobin; Hb S, Hb C, and Hb E are present in various forms of sickle cell disease.

hemolysis—The tearing open of red blood cells, allowing their contents (hemoglobin) to spill out into the fluid part of the blood.

hemolytic anemia—A form of anemia that occurs when red blood cells are destroyed faster than they can be replaced. Sickle cell anemia and beta-thalassemia are examples.

hydroxyurea—An anticancer drug that stimulates increased production of fetal hemoglobin, which can prevent sickling.

jaundice—A yellowing of the skin and whites of the eyes due to an excess of hemoglobin breakdown products; an indication of a blood or liver disorder.

malaria—A disease caused by a microscopic parasite and spread by mosquito bites. It is common in hot regions of the world, such as much of Africa, the Mediterranean region, and the Caribbean.

mutation—A hereditary change in a gene.

recessive trait—A hereditary characteristic whose effects can be observed only if the person has inherited genes for it from both parents.

screening—Testing of large groups of people for a particular disease.

sickle cell—Red blood cell containing an abnormal form of hemoglobin and changing to a crescent or sickle shape under low-oxygen conditions.

sickle cell episode—An episode of intense pain that may require hospitalization.

sickle cell trait—The condition of carrying one gene for sickle cell disease. People with the trait do not have any symptoms of illness.

Sickledex—A test that detects sickle hemoglobin.

sickling—The change of a red blood cell from its usual round, doughnutlike shape to a stiff crescent (sickle) shape.

sodium metabisulfite test—A test for sickling of red blood cells.

stem cells—Undifferentiated bone marrow cells that can give rise to various types of blood cells.

stroke—Damage to the brain due to blockage of brain blood vessels or hemorrhage from torn blood vessels. Death of oxygen-starved tissues may result in learning disabilities, memory loss, paralysis, or death.

thalassemia—A blood disorder in which the synthesis of one of the types of hemoglobin chains is defective. Insufficient hemoglobin is produced (resulting in anemia), and the unaffected chain builds up an excess in the blood.

thalassemia major—The most severe form of thalassemia; also called Cooley's anemia.

Further Reading

Books

Beshore, George. *Sickle Cell Anemia.* New York: Franklin Watts, 1994.

Hill, Shirley A. *Managing Sickle Cell Disease in Low-Income Families.* Philadelphia: Temple University Press, 1994.

Linde, Shirley Motter. *Sickle Cell: A Complete Guide to Prevention and Treatment.* New York: Pavilion, 1972.

Lyon, Jeff, and Peter Gorner. *Altered Fates: Gene Therapy and the Retooling of Human Life.* New York: W. W. Norton & Company, 1995.

Pamphlets and Magazines

The Challenge (quarterly magazine). Howard University Center for Sickle Cell Disease.

Newborn Screening for Sickle Cell Disease and Other Hemoglobinopathies. National Institutes of Health, Consensus Development Conference Statement. April 6–8, 1987.

Sickle Cell Anemia. Public Health Service, National Institutes of Health. Rockville, Md., 1990.

Sickle Cell Anemia. March of Dimes Birth Defects Foundation. White Plains, N.Y., 1989.

Sickle Cell Disease in Newborns and Infants: A Guide for Parents. Public Health Service. Silver Spring, Md., 1993.

Sickle Cell Disease: Screening, Diagnosis, Management, and Counseling in Newborns and Infants. Public Health Service, National Institutes of Health, Clinical Practice Guideline No. 6. Rockville, Md., 1993.

Sickle Cell Fundamentals. National Sickle Cell Disease Program, National Institutes of Health. Bethesda, Md. (Based in part on a permanent exhibit at the Museum of Science and Industry, Chicago, Ill., 1975.)

The Sickle Cell Story. Howard University, Washington, D.C., 1988.

Articles

Associated Press. "Device Is Said to Help Predict Strokes in Sickle Cell Children." *The New York Times,* January 17, 1991, p. B7.

Diamond, Jared. "Blood, Genes, and Malaria." *Natural History,* February 1989, pp. 5, 10–18.

Fackelmann, K. "Drug Wards Off Sickle Cell Attacks." *Science News,* February 4, 1995, p. 68.

Fisher, Lawrence M. "Bottling the Stuff of Dreams." *The New York Times,* June 1, 1995, pp. D1, D6.

Gregg, Sandra. "The Facts About Sickle Cell Anemia." *Essence,* August 1980, pp. 55–56.

Kolata, Gina. "Fetal Hemoglobin Genes Turned On in Adults." *Science,* December 24, 1993, pp. 1295–1296.

Leary, Warren E. "Drug Is Promising in Sickle Cell Test." *The New York Times,* April 12, 1990, p. B10.

———. "Tests Offer First Hope for Treating Cause of Sickle Cell Disease." *The New York Times,* January 14, 1993, p. D25.

———. "Screening of All Newborns Urged for Sickle Cell Disease." *The New York Times,* April 28, 1993, p. C11.

———. "Intractable Pain of Sickle Cell Begins to Yield." *The New York Times,* June 7, 1994, pp. C1, C3.

———. "Childhood Stroke: A Hidden Peril More Common Than Most Think." *The New York Times,* May 17, 1995, p. C11.

Loupe, Diane E. "Breaking the Sickle Cycle." *Science News,* December 2, 1989, pp. 360–362.

McDonald, Jacklyn. "A Day at a Time: Living with Sickle Cell." *Essence,* August 1980, pp. 50–55.

"Sickle Cell Trait: A Risk Factor for Sudden Exertion-Related Death." *Modern Medicine,* March 1988, pp. 136–137.

Tetrault, Sylvia M. "The Student with Sickle Cell Anemia." *Today's Education,* April–May 1981, pp. 52GS–57GS.

Internet Resources

http://www.iacnet.com/health/11063134.htm
(All you need to know about being a carrier of Cooley's Anemia (the thalassemia trait)).

http://www.abanet.it/fondazioneberloni/ing/talassem.htm
(Berloni Foundation against thalassemia).

http://clair.noc.fujita-hu.ac.jp/pathy/Pictures/anemia/thala.html
(micrographs of blood smears in beta-thalassemia).

http://www.cc.columbia.edu/cu/bb/sickle.html
(Sickle Cell Patients Seek Respect, by Loch Adamson).

http://www.ornl.gov/ORNLReviews/rev27-12/text/mnmmain.html
(Building a Better Mouse Model for Sickle Cell Disease, by Jim Pearce).

http://www.noah.cuny.edu/pregnancy/march_of_dimes/birth_defects/siklcell.html
(Sickle Cell Disease: Public Health Information Sheet).

http://isis.nlm.nih.gov/ahcpr/sickle/www/scdptxt.html
(Sickle Cell Disease in Newborns and Infants—A Guide for Parents).

http://www.mgh.harvard.edu/depts/heme-onc/SICKLE.HTM
(Harvard Joint Program in Thalassemia & Sickle Cell Disease).

http://uhs.bsd.uchicago.edu/uhs/topics/sickle.cell.htm
(Sickle Cell Disease: Beyond the Pain—a Comprehensive Approach to Care).

http://www.icondata.com/health/pedbase/files/THALASSE.HTM
(Thalassemia-Beta).

Index

hemoglobin D, 47
hemoglobin E (Hb E),
29, 64
hemoglobin S (Hb S), 26,
29, 44, 46, 59, 81
hemolytic anemia, 30
hepatitis, 54
heredity, 12, 22, 23, 24, 36
Herrick, James B.,
11-12, 92
hospitalization, 18-19, 76
Hurler's syndrome, 87
hydroxyurea, 5, 54, 56,
57, 58, 88, 93

I
immune deficiencies, 85
immunization, 64
infection, 19, 31, 33, 64,
65, 67, 91
Ingram, Vernon, 17, 92
iron, 26, 28
isobutyramide, 58

J
Jackson, Jesse, 7
jaundice, 5, 32
joints, 32, 34, 90

K
Kark, John A., 78

L
learning disabilities, 48
Lee, P., 12, 92
leukemia, 59, 80
life expectancy, 9-10, 79
lipids, 85
liver, 25, 30, 87

M
malaria, 38-40
Maniatis, Thomas, 80, 83
Marchbanks, Vance A., 77
marriage, 74, 90
Massachusetts, 61, 74
Mediterranean, 14, 20,
34, 36, 38
methotrexate, 80, 82
military, 76-78
Moore, Dorothy C., 34

mosquito, 38, 39
mutations, 20, 57

N
naked DNA, 85
National Institutes of
Health, 84
National Sickle Cell
Anemia Control Act,
72, 92
newborn infants, 44, 46, 62
newborn screening, 5,
63, 64, 93
Nixon, Richard, 61

O
ogbanjes, 14
Orchemenos, 71-72
oxygen, 25, 26, 33, 34,
54, 56, 57, 67, 77,
85, 90

P
pain, 5, 9, 19, 30, 32,
33, 53, 67, 90
Pauling, Linus, 15, 47, 92
penicillin, 5, 64, 79, 90, 91
pernicious anemia, 28
Perrine, Susan, 58
placebo, 57
Platt, Orah, 9
pneumonia, 5, 65, 67, 91
polymers, 5
prenatal diagnosis, 5, 51
probability, 23-25

R
Rachmilewitz, Eliezer, 83
recessive gene, 22
red blood cells, 5, 9, 25,
26, 28, 34, 38, 39,
48, 53, 60, 65, 84, 90

S
Salser, Winston, 80
school, 73-74
screening, 8, 61, 62, 63,
64, 74, 79
sickle cell anemia, 8, 12,
22, 24, 26, 80, 90
sickle cell disease, 8, 90

African names for, 14
sickle cell trait, 8, 12, 17,
23, 24, 38, 39, 40,
44, 46, 47, 62, 71,
72, 74, 76, 77, 78,
89, 90, 92
sickle cells, 9, 11, 12, 25,
28, 31, 67
Sickledex, 44, 46
sickler mice, 85
sickling, 5, 17, 44, 48,
57, 77
sodium metabisulfite
test, 44, 46
spleen, 15, 25, 30, 31,
32, 90
statistics, 19-20, 48, 79
stem cells, 60, 87
stress, 33, 67, 90
stroke, 18, 33, 48
surgery, 54
symptoms of sickle cell
anemia, 5, 30, 32, 90
symptoms of
thalassemia, 36

T
Technicon System, 46-
47
tests, 15, 44-51
thalassemia, 34-36, 38,
47, 83
thalassemia intermedia,
36
thalassemia major, 36
thalassemia minor, 36
thymine (T), 81
transplant, 87
transplant rejection, 87
treatment, 53-60

U
ulcers, 32
ultrasound, 48

V
viruses, 85
vitamin B_{12}, 28

W
workplace, 76